"There are lots of books printed and sold that are about leadership. But there are very few that have been written about how to properly lead in the Kingdom of God's work. Dr. Taylor has written out of his personal experience coupled with sound research that will help anyone that desires to lead their organization in a way that is pleasing to God. Research will never take the place of personal experience. Research will, however, complement and support experience in providing an accurate path towards God's way to leadership. If you are interested in knowing how to evaluate someone that you are considering for leadership or what qualifications to look for in a potential leader this book will be of great help to you. I encourage you to learn from Dr. Marshall's experience and research. In this way your organization can grow stronger and avoid the pitfalls, obstacles and issues that are outlined in this great work. Well done Dr. Taylor."

Dr. Roy Bowen
President / Founder
Midwest Bible College
Milwaukee, Wisconsin
www.midwestbiblecollege.org

CHOSEN to LEAD

Divine Kingdom Leadership

By

Marshall Taylor II

ISBN: 978-1-62249-435-4

Published by
The Educational Publisher
Biblio Publishing
BiblioPublishing.com
Columbus, Ohio

Contents

DEDICATION

It is with great pleasure that I dedicate Chosen to Lead to my wife whom I love dearly.

To Cheryl

We have a tremendous testimony of how God brought us together as husband and wife. You are truly the love of my life, and best friend. Through the years, you have been my number one supporter, encourager and intercessor. God has blessed you also as a minister of the gospel to assist me as we bring the gospel of Jesus Christ to as many as God has purposed us to reach. Thank you for your perseverance, endurance, and faithfulness to our marriage and the way in which you have loved and served our 4 beautiful children. You have given me wise counsel, love, and inspiration, and I thank God that he has given me a great gift such as you.

To my late father, Pastor | Evangelist | Dr. Marshall Taylor Sr.

There is so much that I can say about you. You were an instrument in God's hands, and I had the pleasure of watching you carry out God's purpose for your life. You ministered to thousands over the years, and the kingdom of God was advanced through your ministry. You were my first, and primary Bible teacher, and I'll never forget the countless times we've discussed the word of God. When I think of the information that I've accumulated through the years, I know it all started with you. Your favorite word to me was that I had to continue to develop. I thank God for your example and leadership to our family. You took good care of your wife (**my beautiful mother - Heloise**) who taught me while you traveled. You always did your best to make time for your children, me, Vikki, Kay, and our late sister Val. You were a special, unique man sent from God, and I will never forget what you taught our family, and the impact you had on my life. Many times, when you would preach, I recall you asking for **3 more minutes**. Then you would go on to say, "If you don't see me ever again, meet me in the rapture." Dad, I look forward to meeting with you again on that great day. I love you!!

INTRODUCTION

Divine Kingdom Leadership

Foundational text: Matthew 23: 11-12 (King James Version) But he that is greatest among you shall be your servant. And whosoever shall exalt himself shall be abased; and he that shall humble himself shall be exalted.

The primary purpose of this book is to provide pastors and their church leadership staff important Biblical principles that give instructing, Biblical principles and examples of how to lead in God's kingdom.

All leaders must understand why "servant leadership" is so vital to the furtherance of the body of Christ. It is important to understand what is meant by servant leader. While there are other Bible versions that use the term "slave" instead of "servant" in their translations, our research will focus on the word servant out of the King James Version of the Bible. There are too many folks on church leadership teams that don't understand spiritual leadership, and one primary reason is because they're simply not spiritual. Quite frankly, some leaders are not being led by God's spirit. As God's chosen spirit-filled leaders, we are to serve with the right heart and attitude. These characteristics produce unity, peace, and progress. This means that the Pastor or Bishop is God's appointed vessel and leaders that serve on his team must come under the authority, and vision that God has given to the shepherd.

Within a local church for example, God places vision and goals on the pastor's heart by which He leads and directs him. Through this, the church begins to develop, establish and multiply. In addition, the local church leadership must have a servant leadership mentality. This is a major model that Jesus exemplifies in the Bible, and a primary reason that I'm focusing on this subject. I've been involved in 3 church plants over the course of 18 years. Word of Grace Church, Detroit, MI., Grace and Peace Ministries, Sylvania, OH, and Grace and Peace Ministries, Columbus, OH. The experience received from each plant taught me that leadership has much to do with how successful a church develops and the type of culture it will have.

Divine leadership will also develop, as disciples are trained by the servant model of Jesus, in the way that He served. However, it is of great importance that the pastor has a clear vision that is understood throughout the entire leadership team and church. It is a true saying in scripture Proverbs 29:18 *"Where there is no vision, the people perish."* It is imperative that the people he places in leadership catch the pastor's vision, and embrace the direction that God is leading him or her in. If leaders do not support the vision of the pastor in the local church, it will create a barrier, and give place to the devil to cause major hindrances for the entire ministry. A lack of support for the pastor's vision, slows the church's spiritual development process, morale, and motivation. The power of darkness prevents a strong, healthy church establishment. Division or ineffective leadership will allow the enemy to gain an edge in his pursuit of attacking the growth and health of the church or religious organization.

My goal in this reading is to enlighten those who want to lead the right way in God's kingdom through the benefit of my research, observation, and personal experiences. Additionally, it should serve to help them understand the importance of being a servant leader and being of one accord with the entire leadership team. Ephesians 4:3-6 Paul writes, "Endeavoring to keep the unity of the spirit in the bond of peace." A leader within the church should desire to find themselves within a solid state of unity, as the foundation of the church builds. Unity is a must in the church on a continual basis to further the kingdom.

The Bible is clear on what happens in a divisive situation – "Romans 16:17 *"Now I beseech you, brethren, mark them which cause divisions and offences contrary to the doctrine which ye have learned; and avoid them."* Luke 11:17 *"But he, knowing their thoughts, said unto them, every kingdom divided against itself is brought to desolation; and a house divided against a house falleth."*

My prayer is that this collective information will build not only my faith, but other believers to a higher level where our hearts, and actions are lined up with the scriptures. Every leader chosen by God that has worked in the church will be judged by the Lord in how he or she handled responsibilities given to them within the Church of Christ. Effective kingdom leadership means placing a person that demonstrates being "led by the spirit of God" in the right role so that they are positioned to succeed in advancing and serving others in the kingdom.

CHAPTER 1

God's Purpose, Not Yours

"Proverbs 16:9 A man's heart diviseth his way: but the Lord directeth his steps."

As I recall, it was a cold February day in 1984. I was a 12th grader sitting in an early afternoon class at approximately 1pm at Cooley High School in Detroit, Michigan. My teacher was in the middle of teaching, giving instructions, and asking questions of my class. In the middle of her sharing insight on our lesson, I watched her pause and look towards the classroom door. She told our class, "give me a minute and we'll resume." She begins to walk towards the door and opened it to respond to a visitor. The entire class noticed our teacher having a brief discussion with someone as we watched her stand just outside of the door of the room. She then walked back into our classroom and said, Marshall, please grab your things, there's someone who would like to talk to you. So, I begin to grab my books, and school supplies and placed them in my book bag. At the time, I was wondering, what's going on, and why am I being called suddenly to leave the classroom. I wondered who was waiting for me outside of the door. I thought, maybe it was my mother or father. I worried, maybe someone had died etc.

So, I proceeded out of the classroom, and when I saw who was waiting on me, I was in complete shock. It was Lee Corso, the ESPN college football commentator who is well known and respected around the USA and abroad. He was also a famous former college football head coach in the Big Ten league for the Indiana Hoosiers. He completed his coaching career in the professional ranks with the Orlando Renegades, formerly of the United States Football League. Coach Corso shook my hand and introduced himself to me in the hallway area just outside my classroom. He said "Marshall, it's a pleasure to meet you, and I'm visiting to recruit you as a quarterback to Northern Illinois University." He mentioned to me that he had followed my progress during my senior year and had heard great things about me from the former University of Michigan recruiting coordinator and coach, Bob Chimel, who joined Corso's staff. Coach Chimel knew of my career as he recruited me for the Michigan Wolverines as a running back. Coach Corso went on to let me know that before he took a flight in to Detroit, he had already pre-arranged a meeting with my parents at my home, and that he wanted me to jump into his rented car so that we could head to meet them.

First, as we begin to depart from the school, we took a short walk to the main office to sign out of the school with the principal and then jumped in his car to head to my house. As he proceeded to drive me home, he asked several questions pertaining to my goals, and spoke very positively about my future opportunities with him at Northern Illinois.

I couldn't believe what was going on at the time. It was so surreal. I'm suddenly picked up from school by a famous coach who I admired and watched on television my whole childhood. Now, I'm actually talking to him, as we're riding in his car. In route to my home, he also offered me a full ride scholarship to play quarterback at Northern Illinois. At this point, this situation seemed like a dream. I began to thank God for what was happening to me. I had been chosen to lead. I thought to myself, if this coach wants me to come to his school this badly that he would pick me up from school, set up an appointment with my parents, and come to my house, offer me a scholarship, then, I'm going to that school. I was so impressed with Coach Corso visiting me that I rescinded my verbal commitment to attend Rice University in Houston, TX in order to sign a letter of intent to head to Northern Illinois University.

Once we arrived at my home, my mother answered the door with a smile on her face, and my father warmly welcomed coach Corso into our home. We sat in our living room and begin to talk. The coach presented his proposal to my parents about my future education, and why he needed me to sign with his team. We all had a productive, fun, and promising discussion. As a matter of fact, the discussion was also comical. My father was known as a comical man, and an excellent preacher, who regularly traveled as an evangelist. Coach Corso's personality was also extremely comical and colorful. In getting those two together in the room, made for an enjoyable afternoon for my mother and I. We all did so much laughing from the jokes of a comical coach and preacher.

Mr. Corso mentioned to us that I was his number one priority and recruit. Then gave me a plane ticket to visit the university in the next few days. Now, with plane ticket in hand a few days after my family meeting with Coach Corso, the time had arrived for my visit to NIU. I flew into Chicago. I was picked up by a limousine driver. This trip turned out to be a time that I'd never forget. I was treated like a king. Limousine service, fancy restaurants, room service, a 5-star hotel, and everywhere I walked I had an entourage of current & former players, alumni, and coaches surrounding me to make me feel special once I arrived on campus.

During this process of me deciding which college to attend, I certainly was involved in much prayer in my decision making. After much prayer and discussion with my parents, I decided that I wanted to attend Northern Illinois instead of several other colleges who recruited me. One of the reasons that I chose NIU was not only the fact that I was impressed by Coach Corso, but the fact that I had a chance to become the leader of a division 1 football team, which to me was a major benefit in terms of preparation for my future, and a chance to play major college football.

I've always had it in my heart that I wanted to be a leader. As a youngster growing up, I use to watch three older cousins of mine who were brothers; They were superheroes to me. My father was my ultimate superhero spiritually, but my cousins, Edward, Karlton, and Charles were so inspiring because they were amazing scholar athletes. Edward and Karlton taught me how to play quarterback and they certainly led by example. I mean, they were superstars in my book! As a matter of fact, my late uncle Richard who worked with us all would always impress upon me that I had to work hard so that I could become a quarterback in college. He would state to me that I had to be the quarterback because this person was the leader of the team. Whenever I reflect and think back on those times, I continue to realize that God chose me, and was preparing me to become a future leader in His kingdom.

I went on to experience a successful college football career. I was Mid-American Conference freshman of the year, honorable mention All-American, and I was voted the team's MVP (most valuable player) at the end of my senior year season. In addition, I was able to successfully complete my Bachelor of Science degree in economics. My time in school was full of both challenges and memories. I faced many obstacles that seemed impossible to overcome but I'm also grateful for one very specific gift; My sister helped bank rolled my time away from home. Although my parents would send money to me, I never let them know that I had another stream of income coming in from my sister,

Vikki. She had a good job back then, and she would help stock my wardrobe and keep a little cash in my pockets. Those were some good days back then. At the same time, I had to endure many hard times and adversities that would shape me and prepare me for my destiny as a spiritual leader who was committed to be an instrument in God's hands. After completing the first year of my college career, I gained a new head coach. Corso was selected as head coach in the professional ranks, and left town. Although I was disappointed to lose him, the new coach hired to replace him was also an impactful and respected individual. Coach Jerry Pettibone, was an assistant head football coach to Coach Barry Switzer of the powerhouse Oklahoma Sooners football team. This team was considered a #1 ranked team in the nation for much of the 80's and Coach Jerry Pettibone was known as a great coach and the #1 recruiter in the USA during his Oklahoma days. He recruited famous players as Billy Sims, JC Watts, Leroy Selmon, and a host of well-known former all-pro NFL football players. Coach Pettibone was very well respected across the nation. This was important to me because eventually, he had enough confidence in me to name me as his four year starting quarterback, and team captain in my final year of school. As a college senior in my final year, I took this honor seriously because I knew that this coach wouldn't just place anyone in this position. These were golden years for me. I was in a place in my life where it couldn't get better in my mind. I even had plans and dreams of playing in the NFL. I would meet NFL coaches regularly at our practice facility and offices. The NFL scouts and coaches would regularly talk to coach Pettibone and would always say to me that they liked what they saw from me. At the same time, the scouts would always tell me to prepare for a different position for the NFL. Of course, I wasn't the tallest guy you've ever seen. My father wasn't blessed with long legs, and so neither was I. However, the scouts would tell me that I would be great at wide receiver, running back, or a kickoff returner. When I heard this dialogue I didn't care, I just wanted an opportunity to play at the highest level, and to make big bucks. Cha-Ching was what I was thinking. I wasn't thinking about God's kingdom. I only thought about my plan. I didn't realize at the time that God had a plan too. The scripture that comes to mind when I think of these developments in my life is; "Proverbs 16:9 *A man's heart diviseth his way: but the Lord directeth his steps.*" Now as I look back on that time, I realize that God was in the process of redirecting my steps from leading in football, to leading in His Kingdom.

In my last semester of my senior year in college, I had several tryouts and pro days with NFL teams as they evaluated me and several other players on my team. I was in the best shape of my life. My speed and quickness were at a high level. I was ready to be selected in the upcoming draft. I received high marks in my workouts. I signed with a sports agent out of Pittsburgh after going through hearing all kinds of proposals from agencies who wanted to represent me. I was also a baseball player from childhood days and had a tryout with the Chicago Cubs MLB club. I was offered a contract to the rookie team. I didn't jump on it, because I had my mind set on the NFL or the CFL (Canadian Professional Football League). There were options and offers all around me. Things were happening, and life was great. Then, the big turn of events that would forever change my life. This was God beginning to get my attention. My late father would teach that sometimes, God uses negative means to bring about a positive result. So, one Monday morning in early March 1989, coach Pettibone called me into his office. He wanted to meet with me. He saw how hard I was working in the weight room, on the field, and in the gym preparing for the next level. I have an idea that he wanted me to be mentally balanced as to the next steps in my immediate future. He sat me down in his office and said, Marshall, in his southern Oklahoma intonation, I understand and see how hard you're working and preparing for the upcoming NFL football draft. I also understand that you turned down a contract for the rookie team for the Chicago cubs. He went on to say that he respects my decisions, but he wanted to be authentic and clear with me. He wanted me to understand that although I had a wonderful football career in college, it wouldn't guarantee that I would be as marketable to an NFL team. In other words, I excelled at QB in college, but with my stature (size) it wasn't likely that I would play the same position in the pros. I had to plan on playing another position, which would put me behind guys that have played the position from childhood through college. For example, if I wanted to play wide receiver, I would be starting fresh with no experience at this position. NFL coaches would not be excited to dishing out a big contract to someone who is inexperienced at a position, when they are getting paid to win. So now, I was in a dilemma, but still had a legitimate chance to beat the odds.

The 1989 NFL draft was now two weeks away. My body was in tip top condition, until I woke up one Friday morning. I got out of the bed to get on with my day when I noticed a back pain. I figured, oh, it's just sore, and that I would just take the weekend off from lifting and running. Monday of next week came, and the pain didn't go away. I couldn't even touch my toes. I begin to worry because I knew that if I got drafted or picked up as a free agent, I wouldn't be able to perform physically. I began to worry as time got closer, so I contacted a local chiropractor to work on my back so that I could quickly relieve myself of this back issue. After 3 days of treatment from the chiropractor, I noticed that my back didn't get better, but it actually became worse. I was now having problems while just walking. I was very distressed about this and couldn't believe what was happening to me. My agent would call me and share who was interested. I had letters from Tampa Bay Buccaneers, Minnesota Vikings, and Philadelphia Eagles. I was now in full anxiety mode, as I shared with my agent my situation. He told me to just rest, stretch, and continue treatments. However, my back would not heal, it was getting worse and worse.

The NFL draft came, and I didn't get drafted, but my agent Mr. Simmons mentioned that teams were waiting for me to report to their facility for tryouts and physicals for free agency. Mr. Simmons had to honestly disclose my situation in order to even protect his reputation as an NFL certified agent. Needless to say, the teams begin to fade away along with my dreams in April of 1989.

It was a sunny day in May 1989, as I walked across the stage to receive my bachelor's degree in economics. It was a bittersweet day, as my parents, family, and friends celebrated my graduation. My mind was in a paradoxical state. I was happy and sad at the same time. I still didn't know at that time in my life that God was still working on me.

After graduation, I mentioned to my father that I would move home so that I could get expert medical attention so that I could hurry and get myself ready to catch an NFL camp before the start of practices in July 1989. When I arrived back home in Detroit, my father would daily take me from hospital to hospital. He took me to doctor's offices to try to get to the bottom of my sudden back problem. My pain was so bad in June 1989 that I could hardly walk. I had to lay across the seat in the back seat of my father's Cadillac. Every doctor that my father took me to would say, Marshall needs surgery. I heard this over and over again. I thought to myself again, this is unbelievable. I had never hurt my back in my entire life. I never hurt my back playing football, but suddenly when it's time to reach my ultimate goal, my back breaks down on me. I was depressed, distressed, and simply broken. My father saw how down I was but encouraged me to wait to see what happens from my final doctor's appointment. This time with a top chiropractor in Detroit, Michigan.

I completed my final of six doctor visits in nine days. My last appointment, my visit with the chiropractor was the most promising. He mentioned to my father and I in my x-ray consultation that there was a 70% chance that I didn't require surgery, leaving only a 30% chance I would require the surgery that other doctors determined was an inevitability. We decided to go with the diagnosis and rehabilitation plan of the chiropractor and began treatments with him immediately. When the final appointment ended, my father helped me to the back seat of the car and drove me home. As we were riding I was talking to my father and began to express how I was disappointed in God allowing this devastating circumstance to happen to me. I mentioned to him that God was not good to me and that he turned his back on me when I needed him most. I was hurt, confused and depressed as I spoke. I remember my father driving as he responded to me. He said "Be careful in how you speak against God." He said, "I know how badly you want to go pro, but I believe in my observation that God is changing your direction to His will for your life." It was those words he shared with me that turned out to be true. It took me just about 3 weeks to realize that I wouldn't play football anymore. I also didn't think that my back would ever be strong enough again to even jog or be involved in recreational activities. This was the time that I started really focusing on God, July 1989. I begin to seek His will for my life. It was also at this time when I surrendered and told God that I was ready to do what he wanted me to do. I began to give up the sport that I loved, and that was a part of my heart. I gave it up. I came to myself. I said, "It's over". Once I said this, and released it, shortly afterwards was when my back began to heal. In July 1989, I could hardly walk. I gave up hope in ever making professional sports my goal.

In August of 1989, my back returned to full strength, and I was very excited, thanking God for my healing process. I was so enthused that I decided to drive my mother, Heloise, to the Pentecostal Assemblies of the World summer convention. I had no idea what treat I was in store for. This became not only a trip to assist my mother to the convention, while my father was preaching in Washington D.C., but it became the time where God set me on a path for me to meet the love of my life, my wife, Cheryl. Shortly after attending a successful Christian convention, and meeting a foxy young lady, I returned home to Detroit to learn that I had been hired by IBM Corporation in Chicago. The start of my professional career was an exciting prospect, but I felt conflicted as I had no real desire to leave home. I relocated to Chicago in September of 1989. As I searched for what church to attend, I contacted my father to get his advice. He led me to Apostolic Faith Church under the leadership of a new pastor whom my father had great respect. Bishop Horace Smith became my pastor in Chicago, and proved to be a phenomenal, spiritual leader. He was a God-chosen man for this assignment, and I must say that I was inspired by him during my time living in the windy city. Bishop Smith at the time was mentored by another great man of God, Bishop Arthur Brazier, Apostolic Church of God, Chicago. It would be both of these great men who made an indelible impact on my life. After getting started at IBM the fall of 1989, I recall driving home from work one day headed north on Lake Shore Drive. I began to experience God speaking to me while I was in the car. God placed a strong vision in my heart that day, that it was time. Time to begin preparation for the ministry. Once I arrived home, I called my then girlfriend, Cheryl, to tell her the good news about the burning desire on my heart, and how I embraced the call to the ministry to work and become a leader in God's kingdom.

Through my many ups & downs in the natural sense, God simply used my experiences and life lessons to lay a foundation for my future purpose. My corporate experience beyond college years as well as my academic experience attending three colleges has become further development for me when it comes to spiritual leadership. This is my new heart. It's a heart for the ministry. It's a heart to be a part of advancing God's kingdom. I desire to touch someone's heart in Jesus name. Leading in the kingdom of God has become my mission. Establishing and advancing God's kingdom is my purpose. There have been many lessons learned since my college days, and I hope that through the many pastoral experiences, Bible college courses, and research will impact and inspire those who desire to lead in God's kingdom.

CHAPTER 2

The Influence of Divine Kingdom Leadership
A Chosen Instrument of Change

A person called to the ministry as a leader should understand that it really takes much dedication to be qualified, and to determine if someone is qualified to do the work of an ambassador in the kingdom. There are many steps and many tests that must be passed before a candidate is considered for important levels of leadership in the church. The author Paul David Tripp does an incredible job of detailing principles about ambassador work in the kingdom, and how kingdom leaders cannot be self-sufficient. The spiritual leader must be faithful to the calling of God as His instruments of change. I want to now shift our focus to how to be a responsible leader. Once you enter leadership, or when you promote a candidate into leadership, it is vital that the person is responsible, and accountable when it comes to leading God's people. There will be times where you will want to quit, and frustrations will build up to the point where you want to throw in the towel. However, as you endure this race, you will always come to yourself to realize who you are, and whose you are. You will once again realize that not only are the people I'm serving in the process, but you the leader are in process as well. Just because you may have made it to high levels of leadership doesn't mean that God is done developing you.

Many times, God is working on the leader more, and the leader catches more heat than the ones that he is serving. I believe this is how it should be anyhow. Why would you want to be led by someone who has experienced less than you? I wouldn't want that because I wouldn't see how I could significantly grow. This is what leadership should be about. It should be about growth and change. If the leader is accountable, and responsible, then change will take place with his follower. People must understand that ministry and becoming an ambassador of the kingdom is about changing or transforming lives. As leaders, we must live what we read and teach. The change will occur when people learn from you how to deal with the circumstances of life, and how to live a quality of life with Jesus as the head and center of our lives. God humiliates Satan in that he takes unfinished people and uses them to go to other unfinished people and spread the message of God's grace so that He gets every ounce of glory.

One of the major keys to becoming an instrument of change is to target the hearts of the people. "In personal ministry, no matter what the difficulty, the heart is always our target." If you desire to be an effective leader, not only will you target the hearts of people, but it is also of great importance to seek to get to know the people you are trying to influence.

We must ask good questions when talking to them to peel the onion of their lives. It's not enough to know people casually, but we want to really get to know people so that we can determine where change is needed. There is a great foundational scripture for this in Hebrews 4:14-16, *"Seeing then that we have a great high priest, that is passed into the heavens, Jesus the Son of God, let us hold fast our profession. For we have not a high Priest which cannot be touched with the feeling of our infirmities; but was in all points tempted like as we are, yet without sin."*

Thus, we must get to know people so that we can speak the truth in love, which will produce change in their lives. When people begin to see themselves through God's word, the goal is to drive them to repentance. We must pray that our words will expose some things in their lives and that their heart will change to submit to God's word.

We encourage the people by informing them about what God's word says. We provide support, wisdom, and guidance so that they can become biblically accountable. This responsibility of being an ambassador is not about attaining an elite status, but we are to serve with a humble heart. "It is living in a humble, honest, redemptive community with others, loving as Christ has loved, and going beyond the casual to really know people. It is loving others enough to speak the truth to them, helping them to see themselves in the mirror of God's word."

There are three major requirements of the divine kingdom leader that I want to deal with. A person says, "I'm called", now what? Next you must have a field of service, and you must have a God given message. Now let's take a brief look at these three requirements in a little more detail.

THREE REQUIREMENTS FOR ANY PASTOR/SPIRITUAL LEADER:

MUST BE DIRECTLY CALLED BY GOD

There are many Christians, and non-Christians in the world today that have no idea about the calling of God in their lives. For Christians, many believe that the reason that they're saved, and born-again is because there was some type of move that they made, and something that they did in order to come to Christ to receive him into their lives. Even so with non-believers. There have been many occasions where I would witness to them, and they would simply respond by saying, I'm not ready yet to give my life to Christ. One of the most important teachings that I've learned in the Bible, is the doctrine of grace.

The Apostle Paul introduced grace during his ministry and wrote much of the New Testament letters to the church in helping to lay down and communicate what "grace" is all about. You're probably wondering right now, why I am talking about grace, when the subject matter is currently dealing with being directly called by God. The reason being is because first off, a man cannot even begin to work for God in His kingdom unless he had been born again and filled with His Holy Spirit. A major truth in the Bible states that when you do not have Christ's Spirit, then you're none of His. The key here though, is that in order to even be in the discussion of working in God's kingdom a man must be born again of the water and of the spirit in Jesus name. Believers are chosen by God, and redeemed by the blood of Jesus Christ. Acts 4:12 says, Neither is there salvation in any other: for there is none other name under heaven given among men, whereby we must be saved. This is the first step for someone to be involved in spiritual leadership in God's kingdom.

Ephesians 2:8,9 says, *For by grace are ye saved, through faith, and that, not of yourselves, it is a gift.* I want to emphasize "GIFT". This is what "Chosen" is all about. As a matter of fact, Jesus put it this way, in John 6:44, he says, *"No man can come unto me, except the father which hath sent me, draw him in."* This is all a part of being directly CALLED to salvation. To further strengthen this this subject, we must all understand and realize that once a person is adopted into God's family, the Lord will also specifically place on one's heart a vision, or a burning desire to carry out a task in order to advance the kingdom. The scripture that I like to use is Philippians 2:12,13 *"Work out your own salvation with fear and trembling, for it is God that worketh in you both to will and to do, of His good pleasure."* A born-again believer should understand that your steps are ordered by God. He knows your end from the beginning. The Lord knows what your spiritual curriculum will be, even before you start on your journey.

There are many that are surprised at what they're doing in the kingdom, but we should all remember that God is never surprised. As a matter of fact, God is the one who places ideas and vision in our hearts. Circumstances that you experience throughout your lifetime is all for the preparation that you would need for the task that the Lord has planned for you to divinely lead His people. A great example that I can think of is Joseph in the book of Genesis. From the time that Joseph was sold by his brothers, falsely accused of rape, and cast into prison, God had him in the process of preparation for something greater. Had not God permitted Joseph to go through years of trials, he never would have been prepared for the highest office in the land under Pharaoh.

I have come across great leaders in my lifetime thus far, and I must say, when I learn of their story of how God raised them up I can see how sometimes God has to take you down before he raises you up. When I look at my own life, there have been times when I was totally confused about why so many bad things were happening to me. At one point, I felt as if God didn't like me and that I was under His wrath due to suffering that I've experienced in the past. I have had a stretch of 6 or 7 years of just plain old losing in everything I did. I had so many losses that I began to become somewhat bitter, depressed, and miserable. I felt like a failure and started to believe that I was serving God for nothing.

However, I came to realize that I was experiencing what is called the acid test. That was what I was experiencing. After a season of disappointments, losing money, laid off of jobs, setbacks, health issues, and things just not going my way, even in the ministry, I felt useless at this time in the kingdom. Somehow or another, God kept my mind focused, and I had enough motivation to continue searching scriptures until I found a release from everything that I had ever gone through in the previous 6 to 7 years.

I remember on one occasion last summer, I had shared with my wife that I didn't understand my life. Looking back to my youthful years up to 22 years old, mostly everything I did was a success. However, by the time I hit 30 years of age, I began to experience trouble, which were manifold trials. I actually started to think that my life was a big failure, and I became somewhat confused. What I didn't understand was why things wouldn't work out for me. I had watched old college friends from years ago become highly successful in their careers. Guys who would look to me for direction, prayer, and words of wisdom, many of them took off in their careers. These were guys who never even went to church or acknowledged God. When I came to face this, it became so painful and discouraging for me. This is what Asaph talked about in Psalm 73. In Asaph's case, he spoke of the prosperity of the wicked. Going through several years of tragedy after tragedy in my life and family, it wasn't until the death of my father that I really understood what I was dealing with.

My father was 87 years old and God blessed him as an Evangelist and Pastor for over 50 years in the ministry. My heart was severely broken at his loss, even though I knew that he couldn't live forever. However, after driving from Ohio to Michigan to bury him, I stayed in Michigan with my mother to be with her to provide comfort, and to help her with packing items in preparation for her to move to a new location. One day I was cleaning up her bedroom and placing many things in boxes. After a few hours of packing things, I came to an area in the room where my father had several books that he would study. His favorite author was Martyn Lloyd - Jones (1899-1981), of Westminster Chapel, in London, England. I began to get excited about things that my father left that I could use to help me. I was happy to bring so many books home. I brought home at least twenty-five books. I began to read every day, and every time that I would read, I would learn something and thirst for more. But, one day, I began to read a certain scripture that caught my attention and changed my life. In 1 Peter 1:6 Peter writes, *"Wherein ye greatly rejoice, though now for a season, if need be, ye are in heaviness through manifold temptations."* This is the point where I really came to myself. This is the point where I believe that God opened my eyes. I began to understand the tribulation that I had to endure. The teaching in this scripture "IF NEED BE" meaning that if God sees fit that he may allow something to come upon a person to try them. I realized that was my situation. I went through so many manifold trials because it was needed to make me better and develop me.

The trying of my faith is precious, and so much so that God permitted negative things to happen, however, it worked out for my good. The Lord needed to mold me and shape me into the vessel that he ordained me to be. I was inspired by this teaching as I read because it helped me to understand how God works in the lives of His people. Once I understood my dilemma, I simply said within myself, "yes to your will Lord." Although I had felt a call from the Lord many years ago to spread the gospel of Jesus Christ, teach and preach the word of God, I really didn't understand my direct call from God until then. The best way to describe my situation in ministry after graduating from college, is to call it a general call. That is, I knew that God was leading me to do something in the kingdom, but I didn't know specifically what my concentration would be. What I want everyone to know is that God knows how to reveal himself to you in a way where it is clear of what he is calling you to do. This is what is called the "Direct Call". Now that I have this direct call, and realizing it shortly after my father's death, I now have a deep passion, desire, and heart for souls like never before.

I'm on a mission to win souls to Christ. I am also so much more confident and in faith about the sovereignty of God. I know that I am to be a Pastor and an Evangelist who preaches and teaches the gospel of Jesus Christ. I didn't plan it this way, but God simply and directly called me. As a youngster, watching my father pastor, evangelize, and travel, I would always say, I don't want to be a preacher. I ran from the calling, until God stopped my running and began to speak to me through circumstances and through the opening of doors to get my attention that my purpose is to focus on the ministry and that souls needed to be added to the church of God. I am even noticing today how doors are opening for me to preach and teach the gospel of Jesus Christ. I'm also noticing the fact that God is providing resources for me to continue with the direction that I am going in. I must say that I tried to escape from pastoring and planting another church, but the Lord would continue to show me that He wouldn't bless anything I did, until I submitted to His will. Nothing would ever work out for me whenever I pursued the corporate world. I would always face challenges beyond my control, like company wide layoffs. But, when pursuing ministry work and the dream of leading God's people, this is when doors began to open for me to proceed with the spreading of the gospel of Jesus. It is safe to say that now I know that I've been directly called by God to plant a church ministry and to evangelize. That's my course at this time, and the Lord will lead me from this point concerning the future. Essentially, my direct call came from God getting my attention. God knows how to get anyone's attention to operate in His purpose.

Remember Ephesians 2:10, "*We are His workmanship created unto good works where before God has ordained that we should walk in His ways.*" Another way of saying this is according to 1 Corinthians 6:19

"Our bodies are the temple of the Holy Ghost, which ye have of God, and that ye are not your own." The Lord knows how to lead us, he knows how to humble us, and he knows how to change our direction. Just ask Jonah. Jonah wanted to do his own thing and go his separate way, but God intervened, and brought such a humbling that Jonah had no choice but to yield to God's leading. My final example of God getting our attention, and directly calling us is found in the story of Paul in the book of Acts.

This is when he was Saul and on his way to persecute the followers of Jesus. On his way, on the road to Damascus, God blinded him and brought him to his knees in order to get his attention, and to call him in as an instrument in the Redeemer's hand.

This is what I believe the Lord did in my case. Anything that I planned to do, God stripped it until I fell to my knees. Straight out of college, as a former college football player, I was rated as a top six athlete in the country at my position and primed to have an opportunity in the NFL. As I worked hard to achieve a lifelong dream, suddenly, I had a back injury that came out of nowhere that prevented me from walking without pain and having a chance to try out to make an NFL roster. This was the beginning of God stripping me to get my attention. Now, I proudly can say, "Not my will, O Lord, but thy will be done".

MUST HAVE A GOD GIVEN MESSAGE

Once God gives a specific call to a particular person for ministry, He also equips the person to be able to carry out the mission. I believe wholeheartedly that God gives a person a certain message to give to His people. When I analyze my own experience, the moment I felt the calling of God to ministry, and as I look back some twenty-five years ago, it was definitely a general call, because I didn't have enough knowledge to understand what God was doing in my life specifically in ministry. I just had this burning desire to spread the gospel, but didn't know how it would happen, neither did I have the knowledge base to be as effective as I would have liked. My late father taught me something that I will never forget in ministry. I was the type of person who wanted something and wanted it immediately. I will admit that in my younger days, I was more anxious to obtain things than I am today. Especially in the ministry. My father would always say, "Let things develop." Or, he would say, "God has to develop the situation". He frequently talked about the process, and how a slow process leads to a very healthy development. So now, I currently realize that it has taken approximately twenty-five years for me to fully understand my God given message. I refer now again to my teacher, and father, who would tell me that my style would be my own, mixed with a few others that I admire in the ministry.

Men and Women that God has used will make impressions upon the ministry that God has birthed within us. I am a witness that his statement was correct. Wherever I see a video or hear an audio of myself teaching or preaching the word, it is clear to me who had an effect on my life. But, in the meantime, the more experienced I became, the more that I began to see my direction. I believe that my direction and message was shaped by my father, who was my Pastor. God had given him a tremendous gift to evangelize souls all over the country. He was often used in the old days (60's & 70's) to preach in tent revival meetings, councils and conventions. He regularly preached in all kinds of revival meetings and conferences in churches across America and abroad. He was also a Pastor (10 yrs) in the first part of his ministry, and final 20 years of his ministry. He had a testimony of how he use to be involved in racketeering, and corruption that led him to landing in prison.

As his aunt Helen began to minister the word of God to him regularly while he was incarcerated, he gave his life to Christ. He would always share with the people during his sermons, that he knew that it was nothing he ever did to earn or deserve salvation. He also would joke that his mind was elsewhere when the gospel began to be preached to him. As the word of God had a great effect on him, and pricked his heart to receive Jesus, his ministry was birthed some several years later. Many of his over 50 years of ministry entailed the grace of God, and perseverance. It seemed to me that that was his favorite word in the Bible, "Grace". He was also a man given to study and loved the word so much that he enrolled back then, at Detroit Bible College. This is where the Lord made a great impact on his life, because he always speaks about the fact how his college professor focused quite a bit in the book of Romans. It was this Bible book which inspired him the most and provided the foundation of his ministry that he would take abroad and that thousands of souls would come to Christ as a result. His teachings were so powerful, as he had an extra love for the epistles that Paul wrote. As I sat under his teaching, I began to develop a great love as well for the doctrines of grace that Paul presented so brilliantly in the New Testament. In having a solid understanding of the systematic theology of grace, I have been able to sit in discussions with Jehovah's witnesses, Muslims, and other religions in terms of rightly dividing the truth of the word of God. I started to see in my previous 10 years of ministry of how God developed my message. There are some preachers who prefer to mostly teach out of the Old Testament to provide stories that apply to folk's lives. However, I happen to be a preacher that loves to teach out of the New Testament, especially the epistles. This is what seems to come easy for me. Sure, I can tell the stories of the Old Testament, and apply it to a person's life today, however, I get great joy in taking difficult scriptures that seem hard to understand and making it understandable even to a new believer. My favorite subject is, "salvation". I love the doctrines of justification through faith, reconciliation, propitiation, sanctification, predestination, and eschatology. These are some of my favorite subjects. I have noticed thus far in my circles, some of the ministers call me, the grace preacher. I would rather be called, "the Bible preacher."

I always tell them, like the Apostle Paul, it is by the grace of God that I am what I am. I must not end it here though because I don't just stop at the doctrine of grace, but my ministry is also filled with encouragement, empowerment, and motivational speaking as well. To sum this point up, I am the minister that tells how great God is, and what He has done for us. I always tell folks, don't look at your current position in God, from earth upward, but look at your life from heaven downward. When viewing what God has done for you should make a person eternally grateful and humble. My final point is that I do not teach grace as a license to sin, but I use it as Titus did in Titus chapter 2:12 "Grace teaches us that, denying ungodliness and worldly lust, we should live soberly, righteously, and godly, in this present world." The message that God has given me has certainly been a gift to me.

MUST HAVE A FIELD OF SERVICE

Field of service is a gift that God will develop in a person as he prays, studies, and shares the gospel with others. Field of service has much to do with a person's temperament. God gives every man his own temperament which is unique because there's no one person who is exactly like another person. The Lord will take a particular person, and equip that person through personal experiences, and education through one's lifetime. He will use that person for His own benefit to advance His own kingdom. As you work in the kingdom, attempting to win souls, and support different ministry opportunities, you will discover what gifts that God has given specially to you, more than others.

1 Corinthians 12:11 says that *"God gives spiritual gifts to men, dividing severally as he will."* God knows exactly who he wants to use, and for what particular task. It is the Lord that makes this decision as to the field of service. For how can a man pursue a particular field of service when he doesn't have the gift to execute in that ministry? God is the one that calls us into the ministry and equips us with the necessary gifts that it takes to fulfill the ministry that He has called us to. When I look back on the time when I was called, some 25 years ago, I had no idea how God wanted to use me in the kingdom. As a youngster growing up, I would watch my father, mostly as an evangelist, and my late grandfather (Pastor H. J. Hoke), mostly as a pastor. They both served in God's kingdom very well. I witnessed how hard, and passionately they worked to advance the kingdom. I witnessed the love that they had for the people. I watched them travel, study, counsel, and preach the gospel of Jesus to God's people. Although I was so proud of them both, I simply considered them my heroes. I would always mention on a regular basis to my friends that I would never become a minister. I only had intentions of being a basic helper in my local church. Now I realize that it was God who called me to a certain field of service because I never had an interest in what I am doing currently. My field of service is pastoral, and

evangelistic. I am involved in my 3rd and final church plant. I am also currently evangelizing, being invited to preach and teach from church to church.

The Lord certainly opened this door in ministry. I never had planned or expected to be doing what I'm doing in the ministry, but yet God placed the desire, and passion in my heart to want to be a builder in God's kingdom. It did take some time before I knew what my purpose was, but the thing that amazes me is that God will place people in your life to make an impact and will redirect the path that you may be on. For example, I didn't plan to take a Master of Arts course in Biblical Studies with North Carolina College of Theology. I had never planned to complete a Th.D. in Biblical Studies from Midwest Bible College. I didn't know that God would cross my path with Dr. Roy Bowen (President of Midwest Bible College), who has made a significant impact in my life, and ministry. The Lord certainly directed my path, and I realize now that as a person grows in grace, and grows in the word of God, he begins to mature you. As a person becomes more mature, God begins to place vision in your heart and reveals to you what it is that you are supposed to be doing. This even happens in the natural sense. After relocating my family to Columbus, Ohio, I had to make a change into a new industry.

Most of my business career was in the medical industry in pharmaceuticals, and medical surgical products. I was a well experienced consultant with 20 years of experience and always learning and wanting to learn more. But, God placed on my heart through circumstances, to make the decision to relocate to Columbus, Ohio. Now, my next assignment will prove how God takes over, regardless of what my plans or opinions may be. When I arrived to Columbus, my plan was to continue on with my medical career. As I began to start over in a new city, I had goals of landing a pharmaceutical position, or in sales of surgical instruments.

My job search was very intense and seemed to last for two years. I couldn't believe it that I couldn't land a position sooner. With all of the experience that I had, I could not find a company that would hire me in the medical field. I didn't understand why, as I struggled to take care of my family, financially it was difficult. I continued to search, and search, but mentioned to my wife that I would try to find at least a temporary job in the school system. I thought school system, because I figured, at an age close to 50, no company wanted to invest into an old man. In a troubled state, I continued to look for a temporary substitute teaching job to get me by. The good news is that God opened a door for me to work in the schools. A year had gone by, and I still hadn't found my medical career position, as I worked in the schools every day. However, as I worked at different schools every day, and meeting different principals, and superintendents frequently, I started to realize that the school officials thought that I was a rock star in how I dealt with the students. Principals began to pursue my services, offering me long term contracts and more money. I also noticed that I was really enjoying working with the students and making an impact in their lives every day.

After several more months went by, I started to notice that my gift and personality was an excellent fit in the school system and education management. I started to have no desire to go back into the medical field. I started realizing that the Lord was guiding me into purpose. I use the word, purpose, because now that I'm working in the school system, I have tremendous opportunities to touch the lives of families more directly in the name of Jesus.

I'm dealing with children and families who are broken, less fortunate, and educationally in many cases. I'm dealing with folks who need direction, and yet God placed me in the middle of a people that need to know who Jesus is. I used this experience because it is to show how God works. This happens even in the work of the ministry.

A person will have their own plan about what they think they ought to be doing, but as the Lord develops things in a person's life, goals will have to change. And, the person whom God is dealing with will be guided to where their gift is to be used amongst God's people. In many cases, it takes time for God to guide, develop, shape and make us into what we are supposed to be doing. Field of service for a particular person comes from the gifts that God gives to men. God develops those gifts through life experiences. Then God calls a person and positions a person to where he wants them. It's up to the person to have a heart that is totally available to God for His specific use. My field of service through the calling of God, and my development experientially, is to pastor, to evangelize and revive whoever the Lord allows me to touch.

Personal preparation is a key. Once the Lord calls you specifically, it is of great importance for one to work hard to equip himself and study to show himself approved of the Lord. The final component of my field of service in addition to pastoral work, and revival evangelism, is to simply be an ambassador of Christ wherever my feet takes me. My viewpoint on this is that pastoral work is basically within the four walls of leading members at his or her church. I believe pastors should also focus on the community that they reside in as well. My view on revival evangelism is to work outside the four walls of your specific church membership and go wherever God takes you. Travel from place to place, church to church to encourage, motivate, and share the gospel of Jesus Christ to win souls to the kingdom. My final mission regarding field of service is to simply be a witness of Jesus Christ at all times. This is considered an informal service. For example, if I go to the barbershop, I will touch lives. If I'm at my place of work at the school, I will witness and touch lives. Wherever I go, my goal is to be used by the Lord to touch lives in the name of Jesus.

CHAPTER 3

Seminary Learning vs. Learning by Experience

One of the primary reasons that this subject matter is interesting to me, is because out of all the academic knowledge that I've acquired from schools over the course of my entire life, I realized that when I planted my first church, I ran into problems that I had no answer or training for. Once I realized and accepted my calling to the ministry in planting a church, I originally thought to myself that I was born a pastor's son, served as the assistant pastor three years and the fact that I've been in church all of my life. I figured that once I became a church planter pastor, it would be such an easy process in terms of knowing what to do and how things should go.

Before getting started with my church plant, I began to take courses at a local Aenon Bible College to start building a foundation with biblical knowledge. I took courses that were needed to meet the requirements of my local church, and local church council. After 3 years of this coursework in basic ministry 101, I just knew that I was ready to reach the stars. I remember back in the early nineties in Detroit how my former late pastor at the time, whom I had tremendous respect for and learned from, Bishop David L Ellis, would give me and other young ministers an opportunity to conduct the scripture reading on Sunday morning church services. This was huge for me, given the fact that our church was considered a mega church. When I would complete the reading, I would feel like I actually preached because of the pressure of being in front of so many people as a young man. Our pastor also gave me and other young ministers times to teach or preach in other church services, and events as well. Those opportunities were very helpful in our ministerial development process. In the beginning, it was always nerve wrecking, and I knew that I needed so much work, and had so much to learn. By my 5th year as a minister, I figured that all I needed to improve was to learn more of the Bible. Starting off, I thought that if I really knew that Bible, I could be a successful pastor someday. After planting my first church some 12 years after becoming a minister, I deeply believed that I was ready for the assignment. I was read up in the scriptures and had 12 years of building sermons. I knew inside that I was ready for this task.

After 6-8 months into my church plant twelve years later, things weren't going the way that I had expected. The people weren't crowding in for services, and sometime folks didn't show up, and what a humbling experience that was. This was only the beginning of things in the ministry that wasn't taught in seminary. After experiencing issues in my first church plant, I had problems that I had no idea how to solve. Therefore, the book, "What They Didn't Teach You in Seminary", James Emery White grabbed my attention deeply. As a new planting pastor, I was reluctant to take offerings from the folks that would visit for the first few times. My initial thought was to not run people away because of asking for financial support before they got to know me. As a matter of fact, I believe that I didn't take an offering for the first several weeks at the beginning of our church. I didn't realize it then, but I do now that I was so unprepared for things I didn't learn out of the classes I took. I needed to know things like, how to raise money, and why raising support for the church was important for our church budget. My classes didn't teach me about working with church budgets for marketing, staff, and musicians etc. I was simply behind in these areas, primarily because it was my first time in ministry, and I wasn't prepared. Despite my father's 45 plus years of experience in such a blessed ministry, I asked him very little because of my pride. He was out of state regularly, but I wanted him to know and see that I would be able to handle everything. As I look back on my experience back then, I made mistake after mistake with the things I didn't learn in the seminary. My seminary training didn't equip me with hands on church management techniques. I wasn't taught in seminary that I would pour my heart and soul into certain leaders who would later betray me and leave the church. I wasn't aware of the emotional stuff that came with the position.

Once, I had an experience during the Christmas holiday season. My wife and family were in a festive mood, enjoying family and friends. Suddenly, I get a phone call that one of my top leaders informed me that they weren't coming back to the church. Yes, there were some crushing moments that I never expected to deal with. I will say this though. On Sunday morning, my sermon was in context, and exegetically on point. I quickly realized though that it would take more of what I didn't know in order to advance the church. When our church leased our first building, we were doing great for several months until the church hit a time of drops in attendance and folks leaving the church because of personal problems and so forth. Now I was in a position to go into my personal funds in order to meet monthly notes. This caused great distress in my marriage. They didn't tell me about this when I was taking all those courses. I wasn't taught how to do fundraisers. That wasn't my field. My field was the medical surgical field but had entered into an area in my life that I had not much experience. Although I had took classes on the book of Romans, I had no idea about how to develop church culture and establish vision. This was all on the job training. I never realized while building a church, how important time management was with the family. I was a novice in this area at the time, but my heart and mind were so consumed into building the ministry that I put my wife and family in second place. I must say, it got to the point of distress, and problems that I almost lost my family if it hadn't been for experienced pastors stepping in to council with us, and pray us back into harmony. I didn't learn this in seminary. I wasn't taught about being conscious of time management in ministry, especially in dealing with my family. It is safe to say that I truly learned the hard way.

When it comes to pastoral leadership in the church, there is an important element that must be executed properly, or you will spend years attempting to overcome the mess that will be created. In this research, I found how extremely important it is, especially, when planting a church, to not only focus on winning folks into the ministry, but when they get in, ensure that they end up in the right position.

A famous business author Jim Collins wrote in his book about getting the right people on the bus and then into the right seats.

At the beginning, I didn't use the correct methods in evaluating candidates before handing over the keys. I made critical errors in placing unspiritual folks on my leadership team. This caused major divisions in the church and prevented significant growth. One of the primary reasons why is because unqualified, and unspiritual folks were making the decisions to lead a spiritual vision.

What has prepared me now as I move forward is not only experience, but I have acquired critical research and practical information that will enhance my decision-making. The goal is to prevent me from making the same mistakes as I did before. The principle is called "The Five C's." What I will do is list the five C's, and in my own words share some pointers, which were drawn from author James Emery White.

The Five C's are: Character, Competence, Catalytic, Chemistry, and Called.

First, I'll start with **Character**.

Character is the foundational key that you should look for when hiring for certain positions. One cannot hire someone into position with questionable character flaws, for example, a serial predator, or a person who has a problem with misuse of funds. You have to dig as deep as you can to watch for red flags in these areas that have the potential to further damage to your ministry organization. I had an elder in the church, who seemed to have all the qualities that a pastor would love. However, the one thing that I didn't know is that there was a warrant out for his arrest due to a serious crime. Once this problem was made public to the church, it caused great distress, and unrest with folks wondering if we had anyone else on our leadership team with these types of character issues.

The second element to look for is **Competence**. This is the raw ability that the person has to do the job. Look for skills that have been used in other jobs that this person has held. Take a look at his coachability. Even if a person may not have direct experience, if he has the ability to learn, and grasp things quickly this will be helpful. Some folks you will have to train, but as long as they possess good common sense, and a desire to work hard and grasp teachings, it should work out fine.

The third key is **Catalytic**. This area is dealing with great desire, energy, positivity, and the ability to create. In my opinion this is the person that makes others around him better. His presence motivates folks around him. This person is always a good person to be on the leadership team, so pray and watch for a person like this.

The fourth focused key is **Chemistry**. Chemistry has to do with likability. After going through ups and downs, bumps & bruises, and hard-working days, would you still want to go out with this person for an ice cream cone? I notice that many sports teams that win championships always talk about how close the team was, and that they were like family. The bottom line is that if you hire a person and bring them on your team, ensure that you like him, and that others on the team likes the person. This will help to create chemistry.

"**Called** by God" is the final key in what to watch for as you hire someone onto your team. This is an area that can be tricky, and where I made some mistakes. There are some folks who simply want a title, but not the responsibility. There are some folks who simply act like wheat, when they're tares. Many times, the tares put on an act where you think that they're more capable or called than the wheat. There are a couple of ways to test people to see who they really are. One of the ways, I learned from a Milwaukee Pastor, Dr. Bowen, who taught that when people come to you because they say they were called, and have a desire to lead, then that's when you can say, for example, our church needs help in the janitorial area, or we need ushers. Assign them to something that's not so attractive, and you will see what kind of heart they have. Another way you can test a person's calling or commitment is when someone is getting paid. The moment there are temporary financial challenges, the person leaves to get paid at another church. Hiring a person that is called will take prayer, and time to watch closely. A pastor must be very wise in this area or there will be plenty of adversity and resistance to the vision.

One final point on this subject based on research is, hire from within. Many times, when churches need to fill roles in their ministry, they began to look outside for help. When I say outside, they put out ads, and inquire from other churches. This is a dangerous way to bring someone from the outside, or from another church onto your leadership team. The reason why is because you may not know character, competence, catalytic, chemistry, and calling. When you really don't know the five c's on the person that you're bringing in, you could run an incredible risk of disrupting the DNA that you're developing in your ministry. What I mean by this for example, say you bring someone from another church onto your team, and when things don't go the way that they think it should, then they talk around your team, polluting their ears. We did it this way at my old church, and my old church did that better. This behavior only stirs up trouble for the very DNA that you've been working hard to set up on your ministry team. That would be the person that you say, go back to your old church.

Always hire from within because you already know what you're getting. You can always train certain folks and develop them for future positions. It's always good to do that anyway because you never know when key people that are significant to your ministry have to abruptly leave. As a constant developer of your people, you will always have someone to step in to fill the role.

The research in this chapter is so profound because it deals with situations that you never thought of when you were training for the ministry. I believe that the writing of James Emery White should actually be developed as a class in all seminaries that are developing our next generation of leaders. There are so many men that know the Bible, and are excellent teachers and preachers, but when it comes to detecting the Jezebel spirit in your church, who is attempting to dismantle what God has given you to build, it could bring your ministry vision to a halt.

I wasn't taught in seminary that attractive women would approach me for counseling, but really had another agenda, or motive. I wasn't taught in a seminary to prepare my wife for what was coming in terms of getting attacked as the devil would war against her and her husband in a strategic way. I was ignorant of the devices of some women to call meetings with me just in hopes of them being in front of me to get my attention. I had no idea that certain woman in the church would target my wife and use trickery and lies to cause conflict between us to discourage us. That wasn't taught either in seminary. I wasn't prepared for the type of wiles that certain men would perform within our ministry team, and church members in order to gain influence so that when they were ready to pastor, they could influence those to follow him or her. The list goes on and on.

There are times that the leader will need to raise significant dollars to complete a project or reach certain goals to meet obligations. This is the part where faith will be tested. I remember some years ago, our sanctuary was leaking water. After evaluating the root of the problem, I discovered that our church needed an entirely new roof. Something that would cost me thousands. I had no idea what to do in my 5th year of pastoring. I didn't have the necessary funds to carry out the repair. Therefore, prayer is so important. As our members prayed, and search for solutions, the Lord just happened to cross my path with a pastor of the Christian & Missionary Alliance. He actually wanted to talk to me, and when we spoke face to face, he mentioned to me that he had been on his knees praying about who the Lord would place on his heart regarding church repair updates. He offered to help our church at no charge. The men at his church coordinated with other men from various churches in the area to meet at our church to not only fix the roof, but to do other updates within the church as well. Although I didn't have the funds and wasn't prepared to deal with such a sudden problem like this, I began to thank God for placing me on someone's heart. This is why it is so important to have faith that God will see us through.

My final point on this is I had no idea that as a young church planter, it would be a good idea to refresh myself, wife and family every now and then. Getaways, and vacations are a must in order to stay motivated, and re-energized. In learning from experience, I've learned to take my breaks, and be conscious of how my family is holding up.

Now I'd like to focus on how a leader grows his church. This is probably the number one goal of most ministries. This is definitely a subject that wasn't taught in seminary. The research in this area provides great insight to those who are looking to pastor or lead any type of spiritual organization. When a leader steps out and starts a spiritual organization, there's no doubt that most of them have so many great ideas. Although a person may be able to write out his plan on paper, and feels so passionate about his work, it is important to put the spiritual ideas before the natural ideas. Some people think if they have a beautiful property and building, then the people will come. This view is so far from the truth. The area of first focus is that in all things, pray without ceasing for what you want God to do in this ministry. One may have the best building, best equipment, more money, and notoriety, but it doesn't mean that their church will automatically grow. What's needed is the power of prayer. Why? It is because church growth is a spiritual activity. It is a supernatural event that the Lord adds to the church. The second point is partnership. If you want folks to come to your church, you have to invite them. Invite family, friends, neighbors, and co - workers to attend.

You will not grow your church unless your attenders are inviting people.

The third principle is that you must market your organization. Use of social media is relevant and should be used. Signage, is very important, and it is something that must be implemented ASAP. Radio commercials, news ads, and your website must be updated to promote your brand, or vision. You must also have a great place to hold your services. Location is so crucial to growth. Prayer for the proper location is always helpful.

The product must be a quality product. If it is a church, then a pastor must ensure that his sermons and teaching are relevant. The praise singers must be well rehearsed, and well prepared. When folks visit, they must be engaged to the point of wanting to return. Participation is a key. When folks begin to come to the church on a regular basis, it is a good idea to get them plugged in to where the ministry is going. This gives people a sense of belonging and building relationships in connecting within the church.

This principle that pastors and leaders can implement for church growth is called the six P's.

1. Prayer
2. Partnership
3. Promotion
4. Place
5. Product
6. Participation

The fact is, every pastor or leader wants their organization to grow. I believe that if the six P's are implemented properly, the church or organization will grow not only spiritually, but naturally as well.

When the church grows is the time to ensure that you are a strong leader, and one that isn't only concerned about pleasing everyone. The research on this next point is so profound because it prepares pastors to protect against emotional injury. There are so many leaders who desire to be liked. Even I desire for folks to be happy and satisfied with how I lead the ministry. However, you have to realize that you will not please everyone. Attempting to win them over because they're not happy, could end up being a mistake, according to the 10-10-80 rule. The question now becomes, why am I worried about winning over those that may never care for me? When I sit back and think about myself and wonder why I, in the past, have been so concerned about winning certain followers over. I believe the reason why is because fresh out of college, my first career position was a marketing representative for IBM Corporation in Chicago, Illinois. My responsibility was to focus on corporate giant Kraft General Foods, Glenview, Illinois. Further, my primary objective was to ensure that my clients were satisfied, and that their expectations would be exceeded. If they weren't happy, I had to do something to make them happy. This is what shaped my approach for the previous twenty-five years or so. Now as I'm in a leadership role as a pastor, my character is to ensure that everyone in the church is satisfied. However, in my research on the 10-10-80 rule, it has changed my entire outlook on how I should handle myself in this area moving forward. The bottom line is, a leader can't please everybody. Someone is going to not like you or consistently be unhappy no matter what you do.

Let's take a look at the meaning of the 10-10-80 rule. It actually means that ten percent of people the moment they meet you will like you, even days that you're not at your best. It would take so much to shake these from supporting you. The second ten means that ten percent of people will not like you no matter what you do to impress them. This is where many leaders, or pastors get off track, because they're spending so much time attempting to win over people that don't like you regardless of what you do. The 80, these are the folks that will give you a chance to prove that you're qualified and equipped to get the job done.

At first, I was concerned until I researched this 10-10-80 rule. I started to realize that I was dealing with the second ten. I was dealing with folks who will dislike me regardless of how well I lead. The way I see it now is, why worry about the ten percent who do not like me anyway? This is the time to kick the dust off of your feet and move on. This is exactly how I feel, and how I will handle myself moving forward.

My goal now is to concentrate on the first ten percent of those who do like me, and the 80 percent that are suspending judgement. Jesus dealt with this type of situation during His ministry, and author James Emery White mentions that when Jesus sent the party of seventy-two out into the surrounding towns and villages, he was quite clear in His instructions: if you do not find the town receptive, move on. Do not waste your time there. Go to a place where your ministry can take root.

My outlook has changed to the fact that moving forward, I will focus on the ninety percent of folks where I have the chance of receiving their full support in the vision that God has given me. I will never again focus on the ten percent of folks that will not like me anyway.

The final point to this section is that sometimes the 10-10-80 rule will be off a little. For example, if you find yourself being brought in to lead a church over a guy who was the hometown favorite, and the fact that you were being looked to as the change agent. The best thing to do is watch this situation closely, because you could end up with much more than the initial ten percent that don't like you. When the numbers are much higher with those that don't like you in this situation, then it's time to get out of that situation ASAP. This is a set up for you to be extremely unpopular to the people. Always remember, even in disappointing experiences, God will always eventually lead you to the right place at the right time to become the right leader for the right people. To maximize our impact, we simply must love the people, get to know them, and speak God's truth to them about what they need to do to please Him.

CHAPTER 4

Key Principles for Leading God's Church

When it comes to key principles and instructions on how to lead God's church, it has become quite clear to me that Jesus' words to his followers are a message that leadership is an act of service. He was very precise in His teaching and remarkably, Jesus could live out and do what he had taught His disciples. This is what leading by example is all about. In Matthew 20:25-28 *"But Jesus called them unto him, and said, ye know that the princes of the Gentiles exercise dominion over them, and they that are great exercise authority upon them. But it shall not be so among you: but whosoever will be great among you, let him be your minister; And whosoever will be chief among you, let him be your servant: Even as the Son of man came not to be ministered unto, but to minister, and give his life a ransom for many."* To have this type of attitude toward serving in the kingdom, there must be something within you that qualifies one to lead in this manner. God not only lays out what he desires for us to accomplish in His word, but he also equips us with the necessary spirit which should propel our attitude for us to accomplish our goals in Him. I wrote "should propel" our attitude because there are some folks who are equipped with God's spirit, but lack maturity. In other words, they are simply not ready to lead yet. In cases like these, a true child of God must go through a training or development period to increase in their experience, which in many cases is the best teacher. If one doesn't have the correct attitude in ministry, then there is a problem with the heart, and it must be dealt with so that God can bring out our best. Improvement typically happens when one goes through the fire to be tried. A vessel that is mature, and willing to do things God's way, will be led by His spirit. As Romans 8:14 says, *"Those that are led by the spirit of God are the sons of God"*. It is documented in the old covenant that God's people were asked in the law, or the letter, to obey every jot and tittle of his commandments. Breaking any part of the law was breaking the whole law, James 2:10 *"For whosoever shall keep the whole law, and yet offend in one point, he is guilty of all."* My father, who was my teacher, and pastor would say, "In other words, it's like asking a person to live without sin, and without the power of God (Holy Spirit) within you to help you to fulfill this request. In the natural sense, this would be as if God asked someone to paint the ceiling but didn't give them a ladder or paint brush; To tell them to fly like a bird but didn't give them any wings." God hasn't left us hanging without help. Thank God for His grace, in which he gave us His Holy Spirit freely that we may be able to fulfill the righteousness of the law.

So, in this case, he has asked His people to lead by way of spiritual service, and His Spirit proves to be the foundation of being able to accomplish all that God places in our vision to advance His kingdom. Another example that should be shared will give an indication of the importance of being a God-Spirit led leader. Over the course of fifteen years as a church planter I have concluded that there is no better way to understand the magnitude of divine leadership than to have had some key experiences that would validate your understanding.

Examining the leadership decisions I made in four years of gradual growth following our church's planting, I can honestly say that some of these decisions resulted in critical errors. I placed certain folks in positions who had no business in these particular leadership roles. I didn't realize at the time, that the church would grow as far as your leaders were able to lead. I would put folks in key positions because I simply needed the help. They appeared qualified from the outside eye, but from the inside, they simply weren't qualified. However, had I paid more spiritual attention to the fact that this person in a particular key position led from a carnal standpoint rather than spiritual, that they didn't have God's Holy Spirit reigning in their life, it would have saved me from tremendous heartache.

There was always a clash between myself and these leaders because I sought God's direction and viewed things from a spiritual standpoint. I want to be clear that I'm not claiming to be so much more highly spiritual than others. However, the person that I placed in leadership position would always use natural logic concerning matters that we faced and there were always fires to put out. In my research though, I learned there is a difference between servant-leader (spiritual) and self-serving leaders (unspiritual).

JESUS CHRIST, the ultimate servant/leader.

If one wants to lead like Jesus, one of the most important elements to consider is, "Effective leadership starts on the inside." In other words, effective leadership is a matter from the heart of a person. Self-serving leaders are addicted to power and recognition. They are afraid of loss of position. Most self-absorbed leaders will not train their successor. One fact that is true of an effective servant leader, is the fact that they embrace feedback from those they serve under. Another important factor to view is that a self-servant leader will always be a leader who is ego-driven. They're in the work of the ministry for self-gratification, which is the wrong reason. Folks like this boast in the presence of the Lord. Although 1 Corinthians 1:29 speaks against an ego-driven leader, I have personally experienced seeing and knowing leaders in the church who act in this manner. This is the attitude in which the leader is not looking to help others, they're only looking to help themselves. It's called self-promotion, and self-absorption. It is of the utmost importance that leaders in the church understand the doctrine of Grace that the Apostle Paul laid out in the New Testament.

The more that I understand that it is through the grace of God that I am what I am, the more I am humbled at the mercy that was extended to me from the Lord. In the past, I have wondered, "why did God extend his grace towards me?" As I search the scriptures, I find in Ephesians 1:4, that God chose us according to the good pleasure of His own will. If this is surely the case, then why should any individual develop an ego driven type of service in the kingdom? In my research and reading of the "The Servant Leader", by Ken Blanchard, and Phil Hodges, there is a profound example of two different types of hearts in leadership when it comes to ego: The question becomes, what type of ego will you display?

EGO - edging GOD out
EGO - exalting GOD only

When it comes to divine leadership, the answer is simple.

There are some folks who are leaders in the kingdom, in various churches, and religious organizations that don't realize how they're edging God out. Their spiritual priorities are out of line with the word of God. I give several examples here on how God is edged out with leaders who are supposed to be a part of the body of Christ. First example: putting something else in His place as the object of our worship. God is edged out when we rely on other sources for our security and self-sufficiency.

Pride and fear always separate man from God - Proverbs 29:25. One other verse that I believe is very important is Romans 12:3. I'm not giving a Bible study here, but my research shows me how the word addresses folks with a negative ego problem. This verse says in Romans 12:3 *"A man is not to think of himself more highly than he ought to think. But to think soberly."* This my friends, in a small scope, is how God is edged out. Folks that continue on in this manner are obviously producing bad fruit in the kingdom. Many of the folks that edge God out are certainly the ones that will hear these words in the day the Lord reconciles men at judgment. This is mentioned in Matthew 7:23, *"And then will I profess unto them, I never knew you: depart from me, ye workers of iniquity."* If you are a divine kingdom leader, your character should exemplify that you are one who "exalts God only". So, when someone asked if I'm a pastor with an ego, please tell them, yes!! Please count me in the group that "Exalt God Only".

CHAPTER 5

Why a Servant Attitude is Essential

When working to advance the Kingdom of God, it is of great importance not to lead with pride and fear, but with confidence and humility. Of course, that confidence is in God. Pride will always lead you down Satan's road of distraction. This is the cloudy road where one may think that they're on task, but simply headed in another direction other than God's business. When I say cloudy road, an example of this is, I've watched some leaders from the sidelines make some unbelievable decisions that were unspiritual. Although they thought that they were leading by doing the right thing, they didn't realize that they were leading God's people astray. For example, some pastors resort to primarily prosperity preaching, teaching a materialistic gospel. Spiritual teaching takes a back seat. What tends to happen over time is that the people of the church become more carnally minded about their walk with God. This happens when man has great ideas and uses them rather than following God's word and the effective use of prayer.

The leadership that God is looking for is one that will embrace the vision that he gives for His church. So many in leadership forget about their purpose in existing, and purpose for what is supposed to be done.

Our own personal or fleshly ambitions cannot get in the way, or else there will be a need for the Lord to replace you. One of the greatest examples in how Jesus led, was in John 13:3-5 & 13: 12-17. In these passages, Jesus rose from the last supper and wrapped a garment around his waist, then began to wash the feet of His disciples. He then encouraged them to wash one another's feet and stated "blessed" is the man that do these things.

Spiritual Leaders are Hard to Find

It is difficult to find spiritual leaders. One of the primary reasons is because of the heart condition of the leader. The spiritual leader according to Jesus is stated in Mark 10:42-44 *"Whoever wants to be first must be slave of all."* Even though 1 Timothy 3:1 says, *aspiring to leadership is an honorable ambition,* we must realize that it is a big mistake to use ambition where you are the center of being served. The word ambition comes from a Latin word meaning "campaigning for promotion."

The word ambition suggests a variety of elements: social visibility and approval, popularity, peer recognition, the exercise of authority over others. To further strengthen this point, ambitious people, in a sense, enjoy the power that comes with money, prestige, and authority. Jesus had no time for ego driven leaders, or people in general. In this day that we live in, where in the church there is so much politics, and fleshly maneuvering, it makes one wonder is pure ministry taking place.

In the way that Jesus taught about a real leader in His view, it would be a person that never jockeys or campaigns for position. We that are spiritual are to realize that promotion doesn't come from the east, west, north, or south, but promotion comes from the Lord. An important distinction to make here is that although it is good to have ambition, not all ambition is equal. Our ambition should never reach the level where it is before God's purpose. The moment our ambition becomes selfish and for our own profit, is the moment that one begins to steal glory away from God. This is the point where a person is considered out of God's will and not operating in divine spiritual leadership. The book Spiritual Leadership was so informative because it leaves a person with a foundation of how desires, and ambitions should be lined up with God. A great example from research teaches that spiritual leaders are those that follow the pattern of Jesus. When he died for our sins, he had to empty Himself of Himself, and even though He became the God-man, it still showed how the scriptures state that He humbled Himself to become a man, Philippians 2:6-8. For God to empty himself into a man, was a most humbling thing for Him to do. For him to die in order to pay the penalty of mankind and avert the wrath of God was a most merciful thing for him to do. By having the wrath of God averted, it prevents people from heading toward eternal damnation.

What an excellent example that God gave, as he manifested himself in flesh as Jesus Christ. He stooped very low, all so that he could serve mankind. I think of how his enemies spit in His face and beat Him until His body and face were disfigured. Here's the God-man that could just speak a word and would be able to destroy whoever he wanted to, but the Bible indicates that He humbled Himself, and even to the death of the cross which was all on our behalf. He humbled himself because He loved us. He humbled Himself so that He could become the propitiatory sacrifice (substitutionary sacrifice) to pay the penalty for our sins, appeasing the forbearance of God, and averting His wrath. This is what humbles me the most. Leaders that desire to do things God's way should strive to understand the importance of the doctrine of grace. A solid understanding of this, a careful study and meditation of the scriptures most certainly should increase a person's humility. Many leaders will not take the time to study this though. Many would rather attempt only to benefit from exciting rhetoric instead.

This is why I believe it is hard to find good leaders, however, I must say that God showed me that if I was going to have solid leaders, I was going to have to train them, and raise them up. I can say from experience that I've never found a leader that could just come in and function at an efficient capacity. We as leaders must fulfill our responsibility, and train up the next generation of leaders, and keep ourselves updated in God's word.

Most leaders have a viewpoint of earth up (what man has done), rather than, from heaven down (what God has done). Again, what I mean by this, is that most people look at what they've done to get saved, instead of what God has done on their behalf to save them. They forget the scripture in Ephesians 2:8, 9 that states, *"For by grace are ye saved through faith, and that, not of yourselves, it's a gift, lest any man should boast."* This passage in Ephesians makes it so crystal clear that this great salvation was no goodness of our own, but by his mercy, or undeserved favor.

This is why ambition must take a back seat to anyone's personal agenda. We should be so grateful and thankful that God, according to his own will, decided to choose us to be in Him before the foundation of the world. Unfortunately, this is not always the case and it disturbs me to watch leaders in the church become so puffed up that they are no spiritual benefit to the body. What I mean by this is that I've observed from childhood, certain leaders that I've followed. The Lord has allowed many of them such huge platforms for leadership, but the problem is that they become too high, and mighty to deal with ordinary people. Some leaders have turned the ministry into something else. Perhaps they've turned it into a platform for themselves to shine instead of Jesus Christ. In some cases one has to have status, clout or money just to be able to have a conversation or be recognized with certain leaders in charge. A study of the ministry of Jesus shows that he didn't do that but had a heart to serve His people. I've watched certain leaders campaign for position and crave attention. I've watch them enjoy their power in that they operate in a system of folks serving them, when Jesus clearly stated that the greatest among you is the one who is servant among you. When you get leaders who act this way, and whose ambition steals glory from God, this is certainly a person that doesn't understand the sovereignty of God. They ignorantly or irresponsibly forget about how they arrived at the platform that God blessed them with. They begin to have the Nebuchadnezzar spirit mentioned in Daniel 4:30 *"Look at what I have builded."* And that my friends, unfortunately, is the overall attitude of this day: full of boastful and proud folks.

The service in the ministry seems to be at an all-time low, because leaders are so focused on how they can obtain more accolades, power, and pats on the back. This is the trick bag that Satan has them in. It is also very important for me to state the fact that there are many leaders who are carnal simply because they lack the Holy Spirit which dwells on the inside of those who are born again.

Leadership is when a person can influence others for a particular cause. When a leader who ends up in a spiritually required leadership position, but yet he's not spiritual, results in the blind leading the blind unless God supernaturally intervenes the situation. One may ask the question, "how does God intervene a situation like this?" The answer is that God will sometimes intervene situations where the leader is not spiritually led. Take Balaam in Genesis, who was a wicked vessel that God used to convey a message to Israel. Balaam's encouragement to Israel, was to hold on a little longer, and that their God was on the way to help them. So, sometimes God will speak through natural or unspiritual leaders.

At this point, I want to share a chart that was created by the author of Spiritual Leadership, J. Oswald Sanders. I found this information to be significant to share.

The chart below expresses a clear understanding of Spiritual Leadership vs Natural/Unspiritual Leadership:

Natural	Spiritual
Self-confident	Confident in God
Knows men	Also Knows God
Makes own decisions	Seeks God's Will
Ambitious	Humble
Creates methods	Follows God's Example
Enjoys command	Delights in obedience to God
Seeks personal reward	Loves God and others
Independent	Depends on God

The Apostle Paul is one of my favorite spiritual leaders in the Bible, and in my opinion, it wouldn't be fair to not include some insights from Paul. 1 Timothy 3:2-7 Paul writes to Timothy, *"A Bishop then must be blameless, the husband of one wife, vigilant, sober, of good behaviour, given to hospitality, apt to teach; Not given to wine, no striker, not greedy of filthy lucre; but patient, not a brawler, not covetous; One that ruleth well his own house, having his children in subjection with all gravity; (For if a man know not how to rule his own house, how shall he take care of the church of God?) Not a novice, lest being lifted up with pride he fall into the condemnation of the devil. Moreover he must have a good report of them which are without lest he fall into reproach and the snare of the devi. Moreover he must have a good report of them which are without; lest he fall into reproach and the snare of the devil.* These are very important spiritual requirements for an overseer. According to the well-respected A. W. Tozer, who called Paul, "the world's most successful Christian."

Now I would like to briefly give touch points on the qualifications that Paul mentions. First, Social Qualifications. A leader cannot be in the process of trying to lead others spiritually when he has all types of indictments of wrongdoing against him. Moral Qualifications are important in the fact that while others are watching your lifestyle, it is not good for your followers to see you wrapped up in sexual unfaithfulness, drunkenness, or any type of sinful issues in a leader's personal life.

A qualified leader according to Paul's writings, must have a balanced mind, and temperament. He must be a prudent person. A spiritual leader must have good personality qualifications. This means that if you desire to be a spiritual leader, you should not be quick to fight to solve problems, but rather should solve a conflict through reasoning. When it comes to domestic qualifications, the pastor or spiritual leader should be doing a great job with his family. The Bible says, if a leader can't rule his family well, then how can he lead the children of God? One important factor that is a major problem in the church is that pastors and other leaders are so focused in church business, and serving others, that they neglect to serve their families first. In other words, the church work is put before serving the family first. When the family is not the first priority in ministry, there could be some devastating problems that result from this in the form of emotional injury, and lack of direction with the children.

Everyone must realize that when one works for God to advance His kingdom, you immediately become a menace to Satan and his kingdom. The worker is the target of Satan, and the enemy usually starts with the head of the house to break down the family unit. I've seen this issue first hand with many families that I know personally including my own family. The church thrives and builds, but the family is broken. This happens more often than many folks think. Then, when that leader dies, a new leader is seated and the family is left needing counseling because of the emotional hurts and pains they experienced through the years. This is why putting the family in first position of service and attention is a major priority. When a new leader is selected, the church moves on. Now the question becomes, who selects that leader? The simple answer is God. Spiritual leaders are not created by man, synods or churchly assemblies. God alone makes the decisions through initiating and orchestrating how the process will play out behind the scenes or in the spirit. Many times, man thinks that he has strategic ways and answers, but we must realize that man can never usurp the authority and plan of God. The chosen spiritual leader of God is not won by campaigning or marketing efforts, but by the call of God. In addition, God prepares His leaders through their many qualifying experiences, training, studying, test and trials. A qualified God-chosen leader will pass the acid test (tried in the fire). When God is ready, many times he will strategically place this person in the hearts of the people and purposely position them to lead in His kingdom.

God typically works through the overseer (Bishop, Elder) and sometimes boards in order to position His chosen leader. Whatever the process may be in an organization seating the next leader, we must realize that God is sovereign, and knows how to move on the hearts of men to place His chosen leader in position to advance His kingdom agenda. In some cases where proper church government is set up, the Pastor of a particular church will already have in place who would succeed him in leadership, in case of a resignation, or death. Then, the church moves forward. Therefore,

Paul makes it an important qualification to demonstrate that a leader's priorities are in order. When a leader puts his family as his priority, he is ready to lead. This was one of the greatest mistakes that I've made as a young pastor. I was so motivated, excited and thrilled to lead the church that I failed to properly give attention first to my wife and children.

I remember one summer in 2007, I had a deacon who was having tremendous personal problems. One Saturday afternoon, he stopped by my home unexpectedly, while I was in the process of taking my family to the zoo to spend quality time with them. As I spoke to the deacon, he had so much confusion that I had to take extra time to talk him through situations in order that he could gain an understanding to resolve his problems. I talked and talked, and my family continued to attempt to get my attention, pointing at their watches. My discussion with this deacon went so long that it was already 6 o'clock in the evening. I spent six hours with this man before I realized that I blew a perfectly sunny day to serve my family. A week later, this same deacon stopped by my church office on a Sunday after church to report that he had quit being a deacon and decided to leave the church.

As I reflected on the situation, I later realized that he wasn't ready to spiritually serve. I let him know that he had to be accountable to his responsibility in the church, but he wasn't ready to give up some things he had going on in his life. He eventually ended up going to another entirely different church, under a pastor that probably didn't care as deeply about his spiritual journey. It was that life lesson that taught me my grave error in not putting my family first in ministry or anything else. This leads to my final point of the scripture that Paul talks about leadership qualities, and that is maturity. The way that I learned from a huge mistake is I gained experience and maturity. Maturity is Paul's final point. He mentions that it's not a good idea to place a novice in leadership too soon or he may become conceited, and not see the grace of God. If I could give any new pastor advice on placing leaders in position at his own church is to be patient. I learned in a short thirteen years that whenever you place someone in position too fast, it backfires on the entire movement every time, and the person almost always develops a nasty ego problem. The insights that Paul shares in these passages of scripture in 1 Timothy 3:2-7 is considered great spiritual leadership qualities. Now, if these are great spiritual qualities, let's look at what is considered great leadership qualities for a commander in the Army (in a natural sense). The pagan Onosander (a Greek philosopher) described the ideal field commander: "He must be prudently self-controlled, sober, frugal, enduring in toil, intelligent, with love to speak competently, and of good reputation."

So, we should see here that the Apostle in a spiritual sense, has laid down some important spiritual qualities for leadership in the kingdom. If in the natural sense a commander must have certain high qualities, then we should realize in a higher spiritual calling, God is requiring for us to have an attitude of excellence when it comes to serving Him with the right heart and qualities. Before I end this section, I want to share some important scripture points that Peter teaches regarding spiritual leadership.

1 Peter 5:1-7 says, *"The elders which are among you I exhort, who am also an elder, and a witness of the sufferings of Christ, and also a partaker of the glory that shall be revealed: Feed the flock of God which is among you, taking the oversight thereof, not by constraint, but willingly; not for filthy lucre, but of a ready mind; Neither as being lords over God's heritage, but being ensamples to the flock. And when the chief Shepherd shall appear, ye shall receive a crown of glory that fadeth not away. Likewise, ye younger, submit yourselves unto the elder. Yea, all of you be subject one to another, and be clothed with humility: for God resisteth the proud, and giveth grace to the humble. Humble yourselves therefore under the mighty hand of God, that He may exalt you in due time: Casting all your care upon him; for He careth for you."*

The research and scripture reference here clearly shows what leadership is all about. It's not about my personal preferences, and it's not about what money or notoriety that I receive from it, but it is a work of having the heart of God to feed His flock. One of my burdens that I carried for years was becoming concerned about being inadequate in my pastoral role. I truly believe that I felt this way after observing my grandfather, Pastor H J Hoke, Bishop David L Ellis and late father over the years. My father served very well as a pastor, and gifted evangelist, who traveled extensively all over the country touching the lives of God's people for 50 plus years. He also trained my sister Vikki, who is now the pastor of the church he founded, Word of Grace Church in Detroit Michigan. She has become an inspiring leader, a great teacher, and a preacher who also travels as an evangelist. In addition to that, my grandfather was a wonderful and impactful man of God, and great pastor. Through his ministry I saw so many souls give their lives to Christ and develop into solid saints, and leaders. He had outstanding leading daughters (my aunts, my mother Heloise), and sons (my uncles) that he trained, who became great leaders and bishops who were, and still are making an impact in the kingdom. Later in my teens, as my grandfather was reaching retirement age, I made the decision to attend one of my father's friends church. This pastor, Bishop David L Ellis was also so outstanding. As a matter of fact, God divinely blessed his church, as I watched it grow to megachurch status. I watched the powerful impact Bishop David L Ellis had on so many souls and leaders that developed from his ministry. His sons, and many of his elders all turned out to be powerful, impactful leaders in the kingdom of God. God blessed him and his family beyond measure, and I'm grateful that I was able to experience such great moves of God during my time there. I had such great respect for all three men that I sat under that when I began my first church plant, I felt unqualified because of the greatness in leadership that I witnessed from these great men of God. Even though inside I felt God working on my heart to get started in the ministry, the church plant grew to a respectable number of folks who regularly attended. I still felt somewhat inadequate in some areas of my development. Then I came across the verse in Exodus 4:14 where God got angry at Moses because of him feeling inadequate. When God calls us to a particular ministry, he wants us to have faith in Him, and that He's the one who called you and will equip you to lead His people. The way that I lead now is through confidence in God. I trust Him, that He has built me and developed me to be successful in His work. As Peter indicates, *pastors are not to lord over God's flock, but have a heart of love, and humility* 1 Peter 5:5. Not only is that heart of love, forgiveness and compassion needed, but vision is an important aspect that revolves around what God has called you to do. My goal is to be full of faith to receive from God the vision for my life, as it should be for yours. Winston Churchill states "Vision involves optimism and hope. The pessimist sees difficulty in every opportunity. The optimist sees opportunity in every difficulty."

Prayer is essential to the success of the spiritual leader. We should always pray for wisdom, and knowledge. This is one area that I could have done better in earlier in my ministry. God had to take me through tremendous test and trials that forced me to my knees in tears. I learned that talking to God on a regular basis, and spending time with Him, a person gets to know Him better. Luke 6:12 lets us know that Jesus spent nights in prayer. We should do all we can to ensure that our prayer life is continuous. Prayer keeps us on the right path and sharpens our vision.

In order to be a leader who moves people to change, the leader must first move God. We move God by praying without ceasing. It is also a great thing to pray in the spirit. I've seen people become afraid of praying in the spirit or praying in tongues. Many think that it's not Biblical. However, when a person reads the scriptures, believes God and His word, and prays beyond his own thinking, then the Holy Ghost moves within you. You will feel a tremendous charge from within as God blesses you and fills your cup. You will find yourself speaking in tongues, and giving God glory. Too many people fight tongues. Why fight something that happened, is currently happening and is written in the Bible? Embrace it because it is real, and it is God moving by His spirit in your life. There are times where my prayer gets deep into the spirit, where I have tremendous adoration for God, and begin to speak with other tongues as the spirit of God gives me utterance. There is a tremendous spiritual charge that I receive in my soul. It is through continuous prayer that a leader will remain anointed, faithful to God's leading, and spiritual in the way in which they lead. Not only should we pray, but we should display great time management by also reading spiritual books that stimulate our minds and blesses our souls. A.W. Tozer says that it's important to read to stimulate your mind and consecrate yourself before God so that there will be a spiritual impact. He mentioned that knowledge just won't fall from generation to generation, but through reading at least thirty minutes a day.

Our reading shouldn't be so that we can measure our knowledge to exceed someone else, but to spiritually increase our own walk with God. As we prepare ourselves in this manner, we have to remember that God is the one who opens doors to supply you with a platform to be involved with advancing His kingdom.

We don't need any worldly connections, and don't have to campaign, but just staying in prayer and feeding your soul, then watch God use you in a magnificent way to help you, the spiritual leader advance His kingdom by touching other lives in the name of Jesus Christ.

CHAPTER 6

Qualifications of a Spiritual Leader

The Five Point Test

This test for potential leaders is designed for you to understand who is ready for promotion. Who is ready to be on your team to advance God's kingdom. In my opinion, the guidelines shared by Rick Renner provides a filter, to screen out bad character in a person before he is placed into a position of authority. I will list each of the five words separately and will comment on what needs to be done in order to prove worthy leaders.

First, top leaders who are the decision makers must INVESTIGATE. When considering a candidate for leadership, take the time to find out where he came from. If he or she is from another church, ask why they left. Also, contact the other pastor in order to receive pertinent information that can save you from unnecessary headaches.

The second word is INSPECT. Watch closely the potential candidate's life, and his work. This could give you valuable information on who you're dealing with. This person is to be given small assignments to see if he or she is listening to you, and if they will finish on time. It's also important to look into the person's marriage, and their children. If those things are not in order, then there's a red flag to be very careful, and to delay moving forward with this candidate.

The third word is EXPERIMENT. I know from experience now that it is important to ensure that you do not bring a person on your team that will disturb or change the peace and harmony that you have developed. So when you experiment, give the person different levels of responsibility to check how he handles pressure, and if he is timely, and efficient. How is his spiritual life? Does he pray often? Find out if he gives tithes & offerings to the church. Is his heart open to learn, with a good attitude, and does he take sides in conflicts, or stay neutral.

The fourth word is ANALYZE. Now is the time to go over everything that you have recorded with this candidate. You've given him different levels of responsibility, you've tested his timeliness, and coachability. You have also verified his family life and job situation in terms of what kind of person this is. Once you determine that this person gets the thumbs up from you, then the pastor has to make the ultimate decision. The pastor must go into prayer before the Lord in order to make a clear decision. When you make the decision to say yes, DO NOT make a grand announcement in your organization or church. Get the person working but place them on probation.

Finally, the fifth point is to place the candidate on PROBATION, once you decide the person seems to be the right fit, then, move forward with a probation period. Probation is like an engagement before making the ultimate decision to solemnize a marriage. When I decided that I wanted to marry Cheryl, I gave her an engagement ring, and there was a period of time that I had to evaluate to ensure that she would be a good fit for me. I had more time to go out with her, bring her around family and friends to see how well we blended as a couple. The same is with your candidate. Once you decide that this is the person, it's not wise to make the grand announcement, but get them working with the team and see how things go. This is the extra time that you need to evaluate and see firsthand how this person operates with the team. If you notice problems that can end up being significant, then you have caught it in time without the embarrassment of some huge announcement to your church or organization. If you set up a probation for six months, that is enough time to determine if there is a serious red flag situation. If the person is not ok with the probation, then you know that you do not have the right person to join your team.

The final point is to be aware that there will be conflict, where folks on your team will disagree with you. This is why probation time to observe a candidate is so crucial. You have to be aware of how your potential candidate handles conflicts and disagreements with you. "Unfortunately, you can't know what a person will do unless you allow a situation to arise that exposes his weaknesses and strengths."

This is a very cautious approach when it comes to selecting leadership. Again, always remember not to move too fast. Moving too fast with your selection can put you in messes like I was in in my first church plant, where I placed a person in too fast, but had to remove them which was painful and messy. When moving too fast on your selections you end up with folks that work against your vision. I want to end this portion of the research with a quote from Mr. Renner regarding this five-step test process that I believe is a phenomenal quote that should help you make important decisions. When you have done your homework on a person, "You'll be spared the pain of putting people into leadership who look good outwardly but whose hearts are not with you." This is exactly what I had in my first church that I pastored. I had folks that looked really good on my leadership team, but in reality, many of their hearts weren't with me and now I understand why. It's because I moved to fast in placing an unqualified person into a position of authority before they were ripe. I received bitter returns.

GIVING IS ESSENTIAL

When it comes to your potential candidate and how he gives tithes and offerings, Matthew 6:21 says: "*For where your treasure is, there will be your heart also.*" A person's heart is connected to his giving. If your potential leadership candidate is not giving tithes and offerings to the church, then it shows that his heart is not in it enough to even be considered for a leadership role. In addition, if a man tells his wife that he loves her but doesn't give her any money, then he's not demonstrating love to her when it comes to action. A pastor must not be afraid to ask his leaders to give tithes and offerings. If they choose not to, then you know that this person is not a good fit for your leadership staff. This principle is very important because a potential candidate can check out as usable in his evaluation, but when it comes to giving, if he's not a giver then this would disqualify him from being placed in position of leadership. A pastor doesn't need to know details about a person's salary or exact amount he gives but should know that the person is regularly giving to the church.

SPENDING TIME WITH GOD IS A MUST

If you are going to consider placing a potential leader in a position of leadership in your church, it is going to take a spiritual leader who constantly seeks the presence of the Lord. This is what divine kingdom leadership is about. Divine Kingdom Leadership only can be effective if the person being considered for leadership spends time with God frequently. However, it is extremely important not to overlook these principles or you will be headed for bitter returns, and a messy storm that will develop with people who do not fit on your leadership team.

When you have folks that don't embrace what you believe, and don't embrace your vision, you're in for a miserable ride. I'll say this again, I wish that I understood these principles in my first church plant. I was in a situation where folks were coming in to join our church at a fast pace. I was excited because I saw God answering my prayers of sending people to fill our empty pews.

As the church grew, I saw a need for different ministry groups, and there was pressure to try to implement some structure in the church by appointing auxiliary heads. The guidelines that I used to evaluate potential leaders were very shallow, and it caused plenty of problems along the way. There were many headaches from always working out problems on our leadership team. One of my biggest problems was the fact that I had several folks in authority that weren't spiritual enough to be in those roles. Psalm 16:11 says, *"Thou wilt shew me the path of life: in thy presence is the fullness of joy."* This verse can be as a foundational scripture in describing how leaders ought to have a private and consistent worship life. Leading in church is not divine kingdom leadership if the potential candidate doesn't spend time with God. What you do in your private life shines in your public life. When it comes to spiritual leadership, if you're not in the presence of the lord as a pastor, worship leader, or leadership team, then you will be very ineffective, and lacking the anointing when it comes to the power of God resting on you. The person that doesn't spend time with God will have a hard time touching people's lives in a spiritual way.

So, for divine kingdom leadership, the potential leadership candidate must have a healthy private spiritual life. If his spiritual life is strong, you will sense the anointing on this person when they carry on in their gifts. If a person on your leadership team doesn't have the Holy Spirit or anointing on their life, then their leadership on the team will be ineffective, or contrary to the Holy Spirit, which will cause great problems. I had leaders who didn't have a prayer life, and it showed. Many wanted to argue when we had disagreements. There were folks who wouldn't come under authority to leadership, and they would become a cancer on the team by affecting and infecting others on the team. This is a book that had to be written to help pastors because there are so many reports of problems with folks rebelling against authority in the church.

When your potential candidate is being considered, don't be afraid to ask many questions about their home life or private life. Ask how often they pray, and do they pray in the spirit or in tongues. You need to know if they hear from God, and how do they know God is speaking to them. As this principle is about spending time with God, you must understand that it would be impossible to make it through the nine guidelines if they didn't have the Holy Spirit. The Holy Spirit is necessary to be able to fulfill all of the principles that God is calling for in order to divinely lead in His kingdom.

"Without anointing, my messages are simply empty words. But when the anointing comes, those same words become filled with power and life and have the ability to convict a sinner, reprove a believer, encourage one person, and give instructions to another."

This is why spending time with God is so important. If you're not charged up, and led by the spirit, then how can you lead God's people by the spirit? I had several on my leadership team without the anointing of God, and many times I referred to our meetings as flesh meetings. There was no spiritual insight, and this created frustration, and tug of wars with our leadership team that caused great delays in us reaching our goals. As a matter of fact, we went backwards in losing folks, instead of gaining folks because of divisions on the leadership team. This is why this subject is so dear to me and has inspired me to lead using the ten guidelines, five point test, and moving very slowly before I place people in a high level of authority on my leadership team.

DIVINE KINGDOM LEADERSHIP

This subject of divine kingdom leadership is such an important part of God's eternal purpose. Every believer was chosen unto God, and spiritually adopted as sons. Notice that I used the term adopted. This is to let you know that you had nothing to do with the fact that God decided to save you and issue you His spirit freely by his grace. This is the only way that you had the opportunity to become a leader in God's kingdom. To become divine, you must have God's Spirit on the inside. A kingdom leader must be born again of the water and of the spirit according to Ephesians 2:8,9, Acts 2:38, and Acts 2:4.

In this discussion of divine kingdom leadership, I believe that it is critical to understand the definition of each word in our subject matter and analyze this subject to ascertain another aspect of how God works in our lives. So the first question is, what does divine mean? It means something that is of God, or something that is from God.

The way that a person becomes divine is through the gift of salvation. When you read the following scripture concerning salvation, you will see that it is certainly from God. Ephesians 1:3, 4, 5 *"Blessed be the God and father of our Lord Jesus Christ, who hath blessed us with all spiritual blessings in heavenly places in Christ: According as he hath chosen us in him before the foundation of the world, that we should be holy and without blame before him in love: Having predestined us unto the adoption of children by Jesus Christ to himself, according to the good pleasure of his will."* Becoming divine is something that a person can't go get. It is something that comes to them according to the good pleasure of God's will. Wow! What an honor to be equipped with the ability, and opportunity to be qualified to lead in God's kingdom. What an honor. Another scripture reference that I like to use for this point is Ephesians 2:1, *"And ye hath he quickened, who were dead in trespasses, and sins."* The word quickened in the Greek, according to the KJV dictionary means simply to make alive. God imparted life into those who are called believers. This folks is how you become divine, it is because God's spirit resides on the inside of you based on nothing you did; it was by his grace alone. Now, let's define the second word in the KJV Bible dictionary; Kingdom in scripture means, "the government or universal dominion of God, 1 Chronicles 29 & Psalm 145." The King, God, has a domain, and it's in you. Although God is the creator of the universe, the realm of God's kingship is the church, or the body of Christ. This is His kingdom, and His kingdom is steadily growing every day. This kingdom is being advanced through leaders that God equips for His purpose. A great example of this is how Saul in Acts 8, persecuted God's people, or his church. In Acts 9, we see Paul being converted, and transformed into an adopted son of God. Once Paul received the spirit of God, then he was well equipped and able to carry out a high level spiritual task. The same is with you and I. Many of us, before we received God's Spirit on the inside, were used in the secular world as leaders, but now God has converted you, and called you, just as He did Paul for his work and purpose. Rick Renner wrote a book, *If You Were God, Would You Choose You?* In this book, he shared principles, and even indicated that many times God will draw a person that has not much experience in anything, but because the person has a teachable heart, God can take this person a make something great out of him.

The final word in our subject is leadership. I researched the definition of leadership on Google, and it simply states, "the action of leading a group of people or an organization." Spiritual leaders are needed to guide and manage God's people throughout their lifetime. Think about Moses, and how God chose him to lead Israel out of bondage and into the Promised Land. Often God takes our natural qualities, converts us, save us, and then uses us for His kingdom. When I look back on my life as a youngster growing up, I look at from the time that I was in the fourth grade, I was one of the kids who loved show and tell. I couldn't wait to stand in front of the students to share my toy for the day. It actually brought me great joy. I also enjoyed sports at the time of growing up through elementary school. I was on the elementary team where my coach put me in a leadership position as the quarterback on the team. This quarterback position, from the time I was eight years old, all the way through college, I was always the starting quarterback on my teams. In high school, and college, I was picked by my coaches to be the captain of the team. Although I'm referring to sports, the point is that I learned so much about leadership in the natural sense.

There was much learning about life, and principles that I learned regarding work ethic, and leading by example. My goal in life was to be a person who owned his own business. I never thought about being a leader in the ministry, although I was God fearing. As I watched my father as a pastor, and evangelist growing up, I would carry his bags every single week that he had to hit the skys. I recall walking his suitcases to his car, speaking to myself, saying, I would never want to do what he's doing. When family and friends told me that I would be like my dad, I would always say, no way, not me. I just didn't realize God's plan for my life. God took me through great experiences in corporate America, as I've worked for companies like IBM, in Northfield, Illinois. I also spent over 15 years as a medical surgical sales consultant in Michigan, and Ohio. Companies would entrust me to run their businesses out of my home. I would have a couple million dollars' worth of product that I was responsible for, while my boss lived two states over from me. I've won top salesman awards and was involved in numerous training programs all over America.

I never realized that God was using my natural training to prepare me for the spiritual assignment that he had set for me in my future. I went from saying that I would never be a preacher to saying, yes Lord, your will be done. Today, my primary purpose is to pastor the church that God assigns me to, and to manage, and lead His people to him. I desire to win many souls to Christ through the teaching and preaching of the gospel. As I look back, I'm so thankful for all of the experiences that I've had to prepare me for such a time as this, to carry out the assignment of divine kingdom leadership. Therefore, I know that when it comes to divine kingdom leadership, it is a calling. You must be called to divine leadership.

As I researched Rick Renner's guidelines in chapter 8 for those candidates ready for promotion, I find that folks will not be able to get through these guidelines if they don't possess God's spirit. What I embrace regarding the principles and guidelines, is that it is always based upon the foundation of scripture. The scripture that I would use for divine kingdom leadership is, Romans 8:14 *"For as many as are led by the spirit of God, they are the sons of God"* There are so many qualities that are needed to become a divine leader. The qualities are, God's spirit, good attitude, teachable spirit, humble in spirit, heart for God, and willing to work for the cause of souls being led to God.

CHAPTER 7

The Benefits of Change in Spiritual Leadership

This is an element in leadership that's not discussed very much. It is the way that God will often re-direct your path to advance His kingdom. This is true in any type of leadership. One of the biggest mistakes that cost leader's great success is being able to adapt to change. There are times that God is ready to bless you a give increase, but if you are resistant to doing a new thing, it can cost you greater levels of success. For example, there are many pastors that have been praying for their church to grow for years, not only spiritually, but numerical. However, the goal is missed because the leader becomes so set in his ways that he misses and ignores the opportunity to make changes for the better. Mr. Renner says, "You can't experience what God wants to do today while you're still clinging to the past." Some leaders are simply stuck and don't know it. They've always done things a certain way, and they always continue to do it that way. When change is suggested, it is shot down because of the fear of the unknown and what could possibly go wrong. The thinking should be, what could possibly go right. Without change, how can you grow? When it's time for change, this is the point where you must be willing to listen to other ideas. A good leader is a great listener, and someone who is not afraid to make changes.

I remember when I was involved in my second church plant. Our ministry started from scratch, and over a three to four-year period, I began to see the fruits of our labors. The church began to finally grow. One thing I never thought of when it came to growth was the fact that the folks who were there to help me create a foundation, would be greatly challenged by change with newcomers. For an example, you may start off with an amateur singer, musician, or an elder. However, as the church gains notoriety and grows, then well experienced and key people start to come in who are very well qualified or advanced at what they do. This presents a major challenge not only to the pastor, but it causes friction with leaders who were there from the beginning. I knew what our mission, vision and goals were, and finally God began to send those type of people who were gifted and committed enough to help us work towards higher levels of effectiveness. Now the question becomes, how do we handle changes that need to be made.

In my opinion, this was one of the most difficult areas to manage because you have a person who gave their whole heart and soul to help the organization to this point, but then a newcomer arrives who is equipped to take the organization higher. As I looked back on this time there was always someone who was offended because they felt the pressure of being replaced. Often, the feelings of folks will become crushed, and resentment will follow. I've learned that the best thing that can be done is to prepare folks along the way that as growth takes place, change will happen. Sometimes leaders will have to be repositioned. In these sometimes-sensitive cases, it is important to give the person being repositioned enough time to adjust to the change. There will be many cases where the person will not take on the heart of change and will resist. "Whenever one person in your church, ministry, or organization believes his rights are more important than the overall plan or vision, he is no longer a benefit to the organization."

As I look back when I had to replace or reposition someone, many times it was painful for me because I really liked the person and appreciated their heart. However, in these situations, a pastor must do what he has to do to complete the assignment that God has given. A great example of this is how God handled Moses when his time came to be repositioned in Numbers 20:11, 12. As Moses led Israel, God told Moses to speak to the rock, but the Bible says that Moses smote the rock. Although he still got results, he disobeyed God, and it was at this point where God saw fit to make some changes. He told Moses that he wouldn't see the promise land, even though he put in some incredible body of work, and faith, as he led Israel through the years. Now it was Joshua's season to lead.

This is the model we have to follow in regard to leaders needing to make change to continue in advancing

God's purpose. Moses was sad to hear this news, but he handled the change properly and didn't rebel. God still recognized Moses as one of his most cherished prophets that he dealt with face to face. I believe that this message needs to be taught to leaders to help them understand that there will come a day when you will have to move over and repositioned. The ones that handles this well, God will continue to use you mightily in your new position. If the person doesn't handle change well and rebels and won't receive the message, let that indicate they have to be disconnected from the organization immediately before any significant destruction develops. So, one of the major keys to a church or an organization growing is keeping the leadership team open to change.

Preaching the gospel of Jesus Christ, according to Colossians 1:6 will not only cause change within a person so that he produces fruit, but it will also cause the church to grow numerically as well. Always remember that when making a change as a leader, ensure that the change has a purpose. Changing with no real reason will cause your team to become unmotivated, but when they have understanding of the purpose, necessary adjustments become smooth. Leaders who experience great growth are not afraid to delegate authority. There are leaders who simply can't let go of controlling small details in their business. If you are this person, it will be impossible for your business to grow. If the organization is going to grow, the leader will have to focus on different things in order to keep the organization moving forward.

The primary focus in this section is keep on growing and keep on changing. Do not allow any leader on the statt who is a change resistor. This will prevent you from embracing necessary risk. When the opportunity presents itself to obtain more growth, money etc., then go for it. Rick says, there are some leaders, "who would rather than press forward to achieve more, they retreat into a mode of self-preservation. For them, maintaining is more important than gaining." The advice here is to make sure that when you add leaders to your team, they are folks that aren't afraid of change. If the organization is going to grow, then things are going to change.

THE SPIRITUAL LEADER MUST GET ALONG WITH HIS STAFF

Every leader on your team must be able to get along if you're going to have a strong leadership team that will take the organization to high achievements. Mr. Renner shares a case where he had a man on his staff who was incredibly talented and gifted, but he had a very hard time getting along with others. Rick admits to making a mistake in hiring this gentleman too quickly because it turned out that this one talented, and gifted man began to make the team disjointed. The point to grasp here, is always resort to scripture to find answers on a situation. In this particular situation mentioned, is found in first Timothy 1:6 *"From which some having swerved have turned aside unto vain jangling."* These are folks that will get off track and disjointed to the extent that it affects the entire team in a negative way. I had an experience like this in my earlier years of pastoring. We had added to our staff, and I will say, too quickly. I made the mistake of adding a person who was extremely talented and supported the ministry financially where we were able to increase our budgets to get things done. Then, on the other hand there was a disjointed situation. We had increased finances and added an experienced person who was extremely gifted in multiple areas but became an interpersonal cancer in everything she worked on. This was a huge problem for us, however, I wanted to give this leader a chance to turn it around. After talks, prayers and counseling, it seemed that our person only became worse.

This person became so disjointed that it became a cancer that affected, and infected others on the staff. This one person who had all of this talent, yet caused so many issues that our ministry began to decrease in effectiveness and numbers. I realized then that I had to move swiftly or else others on the team would become casualties. That is exactly what happened. Once I made the move to cut off the cancerous person, it affected other good people who had become confused, and started to view me as the bad guy, not realizing that this one person that they worked with was the person causing all the destruction on the team. We had to regroup from this. We had to regress some, as we lost good people, but eventually we were able progress as God settled our leadership team so that we could get back to effectively leading the church. Again, this is

Chosen To Lead

why it is so important to go slow in building your leadership team. It can make or break you. It can increase your process of growth, or it can slow it down dramatically. There will be some folks from time to time that will be disjointed, and not being led by the spirit. If many leaders will admit it, many of us will allow a person with the wrong spirit to join our team and will work contrary to the vision in order to disrupt what God is trying to develop. So, ensure that they are filled with God's spirit, along with being gifted. This person must also be able to take correction. A disjointed person on your team has to be cut off many times because they can't take correction. They're not being led by God's spirit, and end up in rebellion against your leadership.

THE LEADER WITH A TEACHABLE HEART

In this section of our research, it has become clear that one of the quickest ways to learn if your potential leader is ready for promotion is to find out how he or she responds to correction. Not everyone can take correction. Additionally, it is very difficult to give correction, especially when you know the other person whom you care for will become disappointed. However, correction is something that will have to be done or else whatever you're working on will become a failure. I've learned from experience that sometimes when a person is guilty of displaying bad behavior, have made many mistakes, and display a bad attitude, they will resort to making excuses whenever they are confronted about an issue. So many folks are afraid, and ashamed to admit when they're wrong, and will become argumentative, and combative when they are exposed. I have been trying to teach folks to not make a habit of making excuses and ensure that they hear and apply correction with a good attitude. I always let them know that when a person can't own their mistakes, then that person is considered no good for your organization. There are also people who think they know it all and will not take any instructions. This display of character should show any leader that has potential candidates to promote, to slow down greatly. In sports this is the type of attitude that coaches look for and recruit for; The kid who says, "Yes sir."

When one of your staff members have to be corrected, and they decide to argue, defend and protest, then try to be patient and teach them how to receive correction. If they continue to rebel, it means that you've learned quickly that this is a person won't come under your authority. This person doesn't have a teachable heart and will not respect you as the leader when situations become challenging. It is best to show this person the door and release him off of your team immediately, before he poisons the other respectable folks that you have on your team. There's no doubt that there will be accounts where some folks will refuse correction, but instead will argue and won't come under authority. I've never faced this sort of situation, but my experience mostly has been that folks always made excuses and wouldn't own their mistakes. The Bible will never fail us in giving great spiritual wisdom on how to handle these types of circumstances in life.

TRUE COMMITMENT

Timothy was in the same predicament, where he had to deal with difficult people on his staff. He had to write Paul to gain insight on how to deal with this type of problem. In second Timothy 2:24 says, *"And the servant of the Lord must not strive; but be gentle unto all men, apt to teach, patient."*

The idea with this verse is to hear what the Lord is saying to do and do it in a gentle way. Do not argue because you are a servant, and it is for you to faithfully execute what the Lord would have you to do. The job of the leader is to sit down and help the person in need. When that person turns to argue with you and use sharp words to combat you, ensure that you don't fall into the trap of the war of words. This is the time to stay in control and keep your composure to avoid any disrespectful conversation. The keywords for the leader when you're assaulted, or when you come across a person with an unteachable heart, stay calm, gentle, patient, and use wisdom. When you're on the other side of the table, receive correction with humbleness of heart. Listen, and come under authority. Handling these situations in this manner from both sides displays spiritual maturity. I try to discipline myself to not allow any one person to control my emotions. I always make an effort to stay in control, be calm, gentle, but with authority and wisdom. This research is a must for all leaders because you will always come across difficult folks who will try your patience. On the other hand, Satan will always use various schemes to bring you down and bring shame. If we follow the words that Paul gave in second Timothy 2:24, you will always be that leader who applies scriptures in the way that you handle issues.

THE COMMITMENT LEVEL MUST BE OBSERVED

When observing potential leaders, before placing them in high level positions, one of the important elements that must be considered is the level of commitment to the organization. Simply watching folks in action over an extended period of time will tell the story and give you an indication if a particular person will fit the responsibility. There are some people who make themselves valuable to the organization. In other words, if one disappeared, would it be noticeable with the day to day business that goes on.

The key here when observing those who are ready for promotion, is consistency. Does this person work this way on a regular basis, or is this a temporary showcase to gain attention. As a pastor or a business leader who are involved in promotions and staff decisions, it is important to have a sharp eye to determine who's full of hot air, or whose heart is really in moving the business forward.

When you discover a person whom is faithful, then you know that their heart is into what they're doing, but still we have to monitor even what their personal life is like. It is so important to observe a person's personal life, because you really gain an idea what kind of a person you're getting to lead an important role in your organization. This observation advice is also great to use yourself. It's always a good idea to look in the mirror to check your own progress and be honest with yourself. We must realize that sometimes we can't see ourselves, but we need others to give an honest, and accurate assessment of our progress. "How we view ourselves is often not how others view us. Getting a second opinion is sometimes useful (and sometimes painful) in helping us ascertain what we are really contributing to the team."

When considering a candidate, laziness is not an option. You may be considering someone who always talks about being in a key position, but yet slothful, and won't show up to meetings on time. They snap when asked to do extra, or is a constant excuse maker. There is no room for a person like this on your team. The Bible mentions that the slothful servant is wicked, and that he would be cast out into outer darkness. The person must be a worker who is faithful to work hard towards the vision. There are some folks you will not simply know what to do with. Whether to promote them or reduce their responsibility all has to do with if they are lazy. If this person joins your team, then, good luck. It's difficult to reach a high level of success when you have a person that won't go the extra mile. Many times, a person's commitment has to be challenged by assigning them to some lower responsibility and see how they receive it. Always remember that ministry is work. Christ didn't come to be served, but to serve others by giving his life as a ransom for many.

Another big mistake leaders make is overlooking the candidate's attitude. Sometimes leaders get carried away with needing help on the staff and move too quickly without observing the person's attitude. When a person is promoted too fast it causes too many problems. The reason it's an issue is because promotions that come too soon for certain people ends up destroying them because they come to a point where they think too highly of themselves. Romans 12:3 says, *"For I say, through the grace given unto me, to every man that is among you, not to think of himself more highly than he ought to think, but to think soberly, according as God hath dealt to every man the measure of faith."* We need to look for leaders who are serious about what they are doing, and to be humble to the point where they can accept correction, and coaching. This makes for a very productive person.

Something that is very helpful to an organization's success is a person who is a team player; a person who is not so stuck up on his own skills that he doesn't see the value in others. The candidate that's being considered for a high level of responsibility should have the spirit of cooperation. When you have a team full of players who are committed to cooperating with each other in the way that they work, that's a wonderful sign, and shows the genuineness of a person's heart. Proverbs 11:14 says, "*Where no counsel is, the people fall: but in the multitude of counsellors there is safety.*"

There are some folks who are leaders of very successful organizations, but the problem with their success is that it goes right to their heads. They don't feel that they need anyone to keep them grounded or share other great ideas. When considering a candidate to be a department head, it is crucial that this person is not stuck on themselves. It's not good to have a leader who constantly seeks glory. Especially when the Bible says that "*no flesh shall glory in the presence of the Lord*" (1 Corinthians 1:29). It's very difficult to lead a church when you have a person on your team who believes that their point is always right. This is a person who can't be helped and will eventually become a poison on your team. God is asking spiritual leaders to serve, and not to be served. God's leaders don't walk around talking about how great they are. Kingdom leaders are leaders who will be ready to serve with a humble, and teachable heart.

"It's important as a leader to keep this in perspective. You may have a more visible position than others do during this earthly life, but your value to God for eternity is no different than anyone else in His body." Overseers, pastors and leaders must display soberness. When the Bible talks about being sober, it's dealing with the fact of being spiritually mature. When a person is so impressed with himself to the point where it's a distraction, the apostle Paul calls it a flaw within the person. This flaw needs to be corrected before it proves to be a fatal collapse in the organization. This flaw needs to be observed in a person before he is placed in a position of significance. I believe that this particular focus of this research is so very important, because we live in a day where more leaders than ever would rather be a celebrity than a servant. Many don't think about the fact that they will have to face God, and answer to him in the way they lead. As a matter of fact, God will judge the leaders more strictly than everyone else, according to James 3:1. Pastors carry a great deal of authority, and if the position is not put in proper perspective according to scripture, the leader will end up constantly stealing glory from God. The apostle Paul was so secure in his relationship with God that he could care less about special recognition. His primary concern was with rolling up his sleeves and helping people. This is the same example that came from God. He emptied himself as God to become a man, so that he could die for the sins of mankind. He simply came to minister. Spiritual leaders should learn from this example, and always come down to the level of the people to serve them and bless them. Growing up in church, I've witnessed so many leaders doing the opposite of what the Bible says. They have these titles in the church, and then they expect the people to lift them up. This has disturbed me for many years.

Even though leadership positions are important and vital to the church, it is also more important that these leaders humbly lead God's people to produce fruit. I really believe that this subject of servitude must continuously be taught to leaders to fight against pride and haughtiness. These attitudes have no place in kingdom leadership. How can we be sure that we don't promote a person like this? The key is to move slowly and observe this person in many different scenarios. I'm not saying that folks you come across have to be perfect, but I am saying they must have the right teachable heart. A heart that is humble, a heart that understands the grace of God. Whenever I sense that my flesh is rising to the feeling of pride, that's when I quickly remember that I was saved by grace, through faith, and that not of myself, it was a gift. This immediately grounds me every time.

I want to end this part of the focus on looking for the candidate that is faithful to the work of the ministry. It is of great importance that if a candidate is considered faithful, then he is considered rooted and grounded in the word of God. This person should be rock solid and not easily thrown off track. A good scripture guide is based off of 1 Corinthians 15:58, *Paul wrote, "Therefore, my beloved brethren, be ye steadfast, unmovable, always abounding in the work of the Lord, forasmuch as ye know that your labor is not in vain in the Lord."* This means that a leader cannot be promoted if he or she is not reliable. The foundation of the candidate must be solid. Strong and stable candidates are not easily lured easily to other places. As I have pastored in the Northwest Ohio area, I've experienced situations where I've seen leaders that were groomed at my church and were developing very nice. After a few years, before they could fully develop, they were easily lured to another attractive ministry. Their goal was to lead on a much higher level in a more established and larger church. The problem in this scenario is that they went to an entirely different pastor and vision. They uprooted from one place to go to another prematurely. They didn't realize that they had to get re-rooted under a different leadership style, and the possibility of not fitting in. This is what happened to several people who were lured off the course. These are the folks who didn't fully come under authority. These are the folks who didn't leave properly, which means that they weren't faithful. The end result is that they all ended up in no role at all in any of the ministries because God didn't allow it to work out. God blesses faithfulness.

This is why potential leaders have to be slowly tested to find out their commitment level before being placed in a critical position. It is a horrible situation to trust someone in a key position, and they pull out at the wrong time, for the wrong reason. This again, is why we have to move slowly in our selection process.

When Paul uses the term immovable, it means that once God places you in His work, you should be an immovable fixture in what you do. You can't be here, there and everywhere. The leader that you choose to fill an important position must be a person who has made himself essential to the organization. In other words, it would be noticeable if this person suddenly disappeared. This is the question you should ask yourself in regard to a possible candidate. Is he faithful, unmovable, and willing to serve with excellence?

REASONS WHY THE CANDIDATE LEFT HIS PREVIOUS CHURCH

I wish that I would have been counseled in advanced on this section regarding candidates who came to my church from another. However, here are steps to watch for to determine if a person is spiritually mature enough to take on an important leadership role in his church. There were several pointers that I learned to watch for as well. This information is especially important for church planters. If a person left a few previous churches to attend your church, then the chances are that they will leave your church too. This is why it is so important to take your time before promoting someone. As a church planter approximately fifteen years ago, I found that folks would come from other churches and try to change some of my vision to what the other church's vision was. For example, folks would share how their previous praise and worship team did things, and how they had a particular women's ministry, and so on and so forth. I would always respond that we're not them. I would also teach our way that we do things. I've come across people who have gone from church to church for years. This is always a problem. I didn't know this at first. I was just so happy to have more folks show up at our Sunday services, however, I didn't realize how challenging these newcomers could be to the ministry.

Whenever you notice a floater from other churches, it's a sign that there is a spiritual defect with their walk. It is also a good idea to ask their previous pastor why they left. In my first years of church planting, I didn't think about potential problems with some newcomers, I just wanted butts in seats. I recall new people visiting our services, and I would always put a great deal of extra pressure on myself to ensure that we had the best service. Again, I wish someone would have taught me that these floaters are one's that are looking for a perfect church, and there is no perfect church. Churches are imperfect because they are run by imperfect people. We must remember that God doesn't need any help to build His church, and pastors can't worry about being a people pleaser. If God wants certain folks there, he will place it on their hearts, and you will know by their display of faithfulness that this person is the right fit. Most people that are church floaters are those who are over spiritual and have a false sense of the true Holy Spirit. The second problem with folks like this is that they won't come under spiritual authority. When they attend your church, they'll be there for a while, until a challenge comes when they will have to come under your authority. This is why it is so important to take your time in the selection of leaders. I've made terrible mistakes when newcomers started visiting our church. Instead of contacting the previous pastors to find out information, I learned the hard way by placing folks in position, and then needing to remove them after they made a stink of some situations. I had ugly situations in our church for moving too fast to promote someone into leadership.

The first few times that I had bad experiences with newcomers, and then I began to contact pastors to ask about this person, and details about their character. The key word again is faithfulness, or commitment. If the person doesn't have these ingredients and began to be judgmental about what you do, then beware. They become critical of leadership, and refrain from paying tithes to the church. One specific thing that I remember in one of my church plants is that all newcomers who came from other churches, many of them said to me, I've got your back. You're the best pastor I've ever had. When you hear this, be careful because most who said this to me ended up backstabbing me when there were conflicts to work out in the ministry. Now when I hear someone say, I've got your back, I watch even closer, but now from this research, I've learned to simply take my time, or have them work in a less impactful position. For example, if a new person joins your church, and after a few weeks of them attending, now that they want to join the praise and worship team.

The way you will know who they are by testing their heart is how they handle not getting their way. I've placed folks in leadership too quickly and over ninety percent of the time, it came to bite me. I've even had folks to get offended because I disagreed with them on something, and they would storm out of the church. Never chase after anyone who storms out of the church in an emotional meltdown. This is a disaster waiting to happen if you chase them and bring them back to your staff. "Should a person choose to leave, don't chase after him and beg him to come back. If he were really called to be with you, you couldn't chase him away."

There was a mistake made on my part when I first started pastoring. There was a guy that had worked on my staff for a couple of years. Week after week he seemed to be faithful and doing a great job in the ministry. He seemed to be a person that I could count on. He would travel with me to different churches where I was the guest speaker. He was always right by my side. One day though, I found out some information that was very disturbing to me. This elder at my church had been in contact with a new female member at our church, who was a beautiful lady who had a heart for God. She trusted this minister who worked by my side, meanwhile this elder was pursuing this new female member at our church. Neither my wife Cheryl, nor I, knew nothing about it. Then the disturbing news came one day when this person all of a sudden announced that she would not return to any of our church services.

Cheryl and I were baffled and couldn't seem to understand how a woman so excited about our church in two months didn't want to return. During this incredible surprise to my wife and I, we began to notice that the elder that I counted on had been missing in action for a couple of weeks. I began to call him and check on him, but I would never receive a return call. As my wife began to do a follow up call with the lady who left our church, she finally began to open up to Cheryl. She mentioned that the real reason that she left was because of a negative experience, which had to do with the elder, who was supporting me. That's when we figured out that the elder went into hiding and hid to the point where he would never again return my calls. There were two things that I did that now through my research and experience should never happen again.

First, the elder that I worked with shouldn't have been an elder, because if he were true then the entire scenario would have played out differently. The second mistake was that I continued to reach out and call him, asking him to come back, and return to the ministry. As I look back now, I realize that I never should have chased him. After two years went by, that same elder who left attempted to start a church, but it failed in its first year. This is why the lesson is clear to go slowly in your evaluation process. Do not beg folks to come back after they have left the ministry in a disrespectful manner. You're only asking for trouble to chase them down. This showed me that I was chasing after a counterfeit minister who had no business in leadership in the church.

CHAPTER 8

Ten Guidelines to Know Who Is Ready

The first principle that I would like to w*rite about is based on the scripture in 1 Timothy 3:1 "This is a true saying, if a man desires the office of a Bishop, he desireth a good work."* The key word to focus on in this verse is, desire. It's one thing to desire something, but it's another thing to work for it. I always like to refer to one of my favorite study authors, Rick Renner, he writes "Watch out for fantasy chasers. They are the ones who dream of success but never do a thing to achieve it. They sit at home doing nothing significant with their lives. Yet all the while they fantasize about how someday they'll get a big break and success will arrive at their doorstep."

THE DESIRE OF THE SPIRITUAL LEADER

This first principle is a great start as to what to look for in a leader, and to measure if he's ready or not. The key in this subject is not just stopping at desire, but what is the person going to do to achieve their desire, even when it seems impossible. Everyone needs to understand that some desires that you may have will seem unreachable, but when it comes to faith, the Bible says that our father of faith Abraham believed in hope even though the situation did not seem attainable. This principle reminds me of growing up as a youngster in Detroit, MI. As a sixth grader, I remember being a true-blue Michigan Wolverine football fan. I was faithful in watching the games. I knew many of the star players, and loved the coach, who was a legend, Bo Schembechler.

One position that I always watched closely was the quarterback position. This was a dream for me, and a desire for me to become a college football quarterback. I specifically recall the wolverines playing the Wisconsin Badgers in Madison, Wisconsin. I was about ten years old watching the television in the kitchen. Once the game was over and my team won the game, it was from this point that my desire became so great to become what I watched on television. I desired to simply be a college quarterback. One of the pointers that Mr. Renner wrote of regarding this principle was the fact that a person's strong desire must be matched by the ability to work very hard to achieve the goal.

As a young high school football player, I began to have even a stronger desire to be a college quarterback, so I worked hard. By the time I was a senior, I was recruited by my favorite team, the Michigan Wolverines. However, the only problem was that I wasn't recruited as a quarterback, but a running back. This broke my heart. I had the tremendous opportunity to talk face to face with the legendary Bo Schembechler about my recruitment. He explained to me that my height would be a problem with me playing quarterback at Michigan. He told me that I needed to be at least six feet two inches tall. I was only five feet nine inches tall. So, while I considered Michigan, I received another call from another famous coach who arrived at my high school, and then drove me home. He was the new coach at Northern Illinois University. Coach Lee Corso, the popular ESPN commentator for modern day college football. Coach Corso explained to me that he was interested in me playing quarterback for his team, and that he didn't care if I was a short guy. He believed, based on my experience in high school that I could do it. His words to me were, "if Doug Flutie (famous Boston College QB, who was short in stature) could do it, then you can do it too." I was so inspired by him, I committed to Northern Illinois.

Now here's where the desire had to kick in, because when I arrived at the school for my first football camp, I saw 5 other quarterbacks on the team, and they were all over six foot tall. A few of them were six feet four inches tall. I thought to myself, oh boy! However, as I began to practice with the team, I noticed that my talent level wasn't far off from the other guys. This too, inspired me, and that's when my desire to work kicked in. I thought to myself, the other quarterbacks may be taller than me, but that doesn't mean that they can out work me for the job. I desired this position of starting quarterback so badly that I worked tirelessly to win the job. By the end of the first season, I'd won the starting quarterback job over the other five guys. This is what Rick Renner was writing about. It's the desire to want to reach a goal to the point where your work ethic exceeds your desire. The Lord God blessed me to have such a wonderful career as a four-year starting quarterback for a first-class division one football program in college. It's the same principle when having the desire to work for God in the ministry with whatever He calls you to do.

There are so many people that have certain desires to lead, but their desires are really predicated on having a title. The work ethic is not there. When seeing a person like this, he or she is not ready for promotion. Something else that I picked up from this research is the fact that there are folks that have carnal ambition, and spiritual ambition. Carnal ambition is what develops as the spirit of competition within the church organization. There are carnal leaders that will attempt to block a person that God wants to use, because of being afraid that that person will exceed their success. This is something that doesn't belong in the church, but it is experienced more often than it should. Spiritual ambition is what's needed in the church. Unity, and being on one accord to carry out the purpose of God. Spreading the gospel of Jesus Christ, and working diligently to promote, and advance the kingdom should be what leaders stand for. This is what is called spiritual ambition.

Another important point is when watching and observing a person for promotion, look at how he or she operates in their personal life. Again, if they're lazy, slow and sloppy outside of ministry, and in their personal life, then this should give you an idea what type of desire this person really has. The person must lead with excellence.

I've found that when you watch a person close enough, you'll be able to see what their inner drive is like. Are they on time for meetings, are they unconcerned or detached. There will always be many obstacles to overcome, but if your desire is strong enough to overcome hindrances, you'll be a strategic instrument in God's hands.

My final point on this subject is, watching how a person deals with adversity. It's all about how adversity is handled, but when you find the person that is spiritual, and has spiritual ambition, and refuses to quit, this person will reach many high goals by advancing the kingdom. A strong spiritual desire, spiritual ambition, and trust in God will always produce a person who is ready for promotion.

CHAPTER 9

Communication & Marriage In Leadership

The Power of Prayer

Communication is key to getting your point across and getting things done. When a person is leading others, understanding each other is one of the most key facts about transferring information. Leadership is communication. That may sound too simple to be true, but it's a fact that good leaders and bad leaders are distinguished by how well they communicate. The learning point here is that if your team is not functioning properly, and not carrying out plans the way you would want, then it means that there was a breakdown in communication. A leader's expectations must be very clear, or else, the listener will not meet your expectations. When there is no efficient communication, conflict and problems develop to the point of becoming nonproductive. Misunderstandings between leaders and those they lead can be common, but they can also be eliminated by ensuring that every step of instructions are clear so that there aren't any excuses about what is to be done. So, when there is a breakdown in communication on a leadership team, it's either the communicators fault or the listeners fault. It's the communicator who is at fault if directions or details are not laid out clearly and in detail. The way to know if you have a good listener is to watch how he completes his assignments.

If mostly everyone else on your leadership staff gets things right most of the time, but one person continues to be off track, then there's a listening problem. In James 1:19, the Bible says, *"Wherefore, my beloved brethren, let every man be swift to hear, slow to speak, slow to wrath."* This lets us know how important listening should be. It should come in first place, ahead of talking. You can tell a good listener, because he'll ask follow up questions, like, is it fair to say, or, is this what you were trying to tell me? A good listener will wait until the other person is finished talking before he shames himself in speaking out before the communicator is done communicating. This principle is based on Proverbs 18:13 *"he that answereth a matter before he heareth it, it is folly and shame unto him."*

When it comes to building a church, it is just as important to be anointed as it is a communicator. You may get a message across, but are you really connecting with the people? There are so many talented, and gifted people that don't know how to effectively communicate and share their ideas and visions. How can anyone know about you, if you do not share what you know, who you are or what you stand for? So, when considering a person for leadership, it is always best to put them in a position that they can report directly to you.

The position that you place them in should not be anything significant enough to cause a big stir in your organization if it doesn't work out for them to be leaders. However, it is a good idea to have them report to you first and watch how they communicate with you. You will be able to tell if their leadership is spiritual and if their communication is clear. This is an important factor to determine before placing them into significant leadership. For example, the Bible is communicating clearly when it talks about the effects of sin, penalty of sin, how to be delivered from sin, how to be forgiven of sin, about heaven, hell and the Holy Spirit.

On issues of vital importance, the Bible is clear. God left no room for us to misinterpret what He says. It is possible to know exactly what God thinks about these central issues because His word has vividly spelled it out for us. There are many that are still confused about what God is saying in the Bible, and the reason they are confused is because they are not listening. Some folks aren't taking the time to hear God out, and cut him off on a regular basis, before the completion of truth is fully communicated. As a matter of fact, I have folks that I will witness to. They have serious questions about the Bible, and in many cases, believe that they can't rely on the Bible because they believe that the Bible was meddled with by man in order to manipulate people into false influence. So what certain people will do is take several passages in the Bible and argue and attempt to present facts on why the Bible isn't completely full of truth.

Whenever I talk to folks like this, I always use a saying that my father taught me. He would tell people "Before you check me off, please check me out!" What he was saying was, give me a chance to communicate, and present certain doctrines of the Bible so that you can clearly see that the word of God is communicating truth in its entirety. In other words, he needed people to be good listeners in order to prevent them from being confused and losing hope in God. So, in spiritual leadership when one is looking to promote someone, take your time and move slowly because if a person is promoted too quickly, it could cause major problems in the ministry, and people can be seriously hurt in the process.

THE HOME LIFE OF A PROSPECTIVE LEADER

In this thorough research on how to evaluate a potential candidate for a top position in your organization, it is so very vital to have an idea of what his or her personal life is like. I've had many experiences in life where people will show in public that they are jewels, when really the real person they are behind closed doors is ungodly. This is why it is so important to move slowly in placing leaders in top positions in ministry. What happens in a person's private life affects his public ministry. What I really like about some of the guidelines in this chapter is that it is a solid evaluation process based upon scripture. For example, this guideline pertains to a person's private life, the Bible states in First Timothy 3:4,5 "*One that ruleth well his own house, having his children in subjection with all gravity; (For if a man knows not how to rule his own house, how shall he take care of the church of God?)"*

It is important to understand that this guideline is not to be used to attempt to eliminate candidates, but to have a better understanding of a person's character when it comes to patience, kindness, selflessness, faithfulness and other qualities. God is zeroing in on a person's heart. It is also just as important that if you do find flaws, and you will find flaws because no one person is perfect, to observe if this person has a teachable heart.

In my own personal experience, I had a leader in a top position who seemed to exemplify terrific character in most of the areas listed above. He seemed to have his personal life in order to the point where he seemed to be developing a strong family base. After watching him for a little over a year, I had believed he was ready. His public display was almost flawless. His private life seemed steady, and his only major challenge seemed to be obtaining a better higher paying job. However, what's in private will almost always show up publicly. This leader that I trusted in was involved in undercover criminal activity. When it came to light, it blew my mind because he was so clever in hiding major flaws that he had. Therefore, in selecting potential leaders, you can't move fast, but you have to move slowly. In your moving slow will protect you as the top leader, and others major hurt and future pain. You should look not for a candidate free of problems, but for one who knows how to turn to God and manage life's challenges according to scripture.

The primary message to get across here is that your personal life will certainly influence your public life. Folks are observing your life, and how you lead your family. If you are not getting the job done with your own family, how can you instruct others regarding their family? You simply won't have the respect or leverage to influence others if they see that your life is a wreck in private. There are many pastors who are human and have problems in their personal lives. I've had many problems to deal with in my own personal life. Especially when you're involved in divine kingdom leadership. The attack from Satan is intense, and if you don't have on the whole armor of God, it will be difficult to overcome the onslaught of attacks that come your way. I believe that the key to dealing with real life attacks from Satan is to pray in the spirit and ask God for a measure of wisdom in order to know how to deal with your problem according to scripture. When wisdom is exercised by the spirit of God, it makes it difficult for the enemy to be effective in his attacks. If others see you attacked personally, and it's not handled properly by you according to scripture, it will certainly affect your witness in a negative way. You will lose respect, credibility, and your words of influence will become powerless and ineffective.

On the other hand, when your church, business or organization observe the attacks on your life, it is also important not to try to hide your emotions, and certain challenges and obstacles you face. The reason being is that you can become a huge testimony to others watching you and trying to figure out and pray how to overcome obstacles in their own lives. This is what the apostle Paul did as a leader. He was right before the people with many challenges, obstacles, and persecution that he faced almost on a regular basis. Paul was able to turn his persecutions into teaching moments for those whom God called him to lead. Paul showed persistence. To keep going and going on with his assignment regardless of the situation that he faced. As a pastor or the leader, you are the example to the people following you, how to walk in faith. Folks need to witness that you are not perfect, but will face attacks personally, and in your family, business or church. They need to see this and watch how you handle yourself. The result is the key to leading by example. The people must see that walking in faith and facing challenges according to scripture that the result will always turn out in your favor. This is when a leader has a strong voice. A person can't teach authoritatively about marriage if his marriage is a mess. A person can't have a strong voice in finances if their finances are out of control. When a leader walks according to what he preaches, it gives backing, and credibility to what he says to his followers. I recall when I first started preaching at the age of 25.

I was a few years out of college, with a great job with IBM. I had a brand new red sports car, and a beautiful wife that also had a corporate position at Discover

Card headquarters outside of Chicago, Illinois. I was asked one Sunday to minister at a church that had a crowd of three hundred folks. Although I was nervous in my beginning stages to preach in front of a seasoned group of folks, I was just grateful to speak at an established ministry. As I ministered that Sunday morning, I remember talking about faith. I was very emphatic about getting across the fact that you must have strong faith even when you feel as though you're in jeopardy. As I looked into some folk's eyes, I saw doubt, fear and people who really needed a revival. As the church service ended, the pastor shook my hand and thanked me for an on-time message that his folks needed. As I jumped into my car with my wife, I began to share with her why don't folks have stronger faith, and why are people wavering when it comes to faith in God. I began to let the people have it!

You see, I didn't realize that I was just getting started in ministry, and that things were going very well for me in all facets of my life at the time. It wasn't until about 7 years later, my wife and I, along with our children began to experience a storm of heavy issues that we were facing. I noticed some days that I was so heavy that I began to be greatly discouraged. I had been in an area in my life where I was able to build a very nice home from the salary I made in the medical industry. However, I never saw the day coming that I would lose my job because of company wide cutbacks and layoffs. My challenge became, how am I going to pay my mortgage?, How will I pay my car note?, and how would I be able to replace this high salary quickly? I would go to church to try to get a word from my pastor, and one Sunday morning God reminded me of the sermon I had preached to some folks just seven years ago when they had seemed troubled. Now I was the one troubled and looking to have my faith boosted. That's when I realized that leaders have to go through experiences too, and sometimes very tough situations if you're going to lead at a high level. How could I really help someone else in an effective way when I haven't had certain experiences? Preaching and teaching will always be very effective when the pastor has experienced tough challenges and God brought him out. It also gives him credibility to teach others how to deal with certain situations because of the experience and faith that had to be applied in his difficult time. I believe that it is vital to live what we preach and teach. The people are looking for authentic leaders who are walking the talk. There are no perfect leaders, there are no perfect marriages, and there is no one without flaws. However, Paul teaches in First Timothy 3:2 that, *"A Bishop then must be blameless, the husband of one wife, vigilant, sober, of good behavior, given to hospitality, apt to teach;"* The word blameless in the scripture doesn't mean to be perfect, but it's talking about a person that has certain problems that are publicly known to the point where his witness is destroyed, and the people won't hear him. In other words, it wouldn't be a good idea for me to do a series on finances, when I just went through a horrific bankruptcy. Or, it wouldn't be a good idea to promote that I'm counseling married couples when my own marriage didn't last and didn't display a good example. So blameless here means problems that won't hinder your witness to others who are following you.

The principles that the apostle Paul laid out, gives much substance to what to look for in considering a potential leader to have a prominent role in your church, business or organization. The apostle spoke of a leader that has a home life that is in order. Does the person keep his property in good shape? Is his relationship solid with his spouse? Are his children in order? Are his finances in order? These are important questions to consider when making a decision if someone is ready or not. Remember, you can gather so much information about a person from analyzing their children. If their children are well behaved, and carry themselves in a respectable manner, you can get a good idea of what kind of leader you have. Why? It is because, as a soft rule, children are a reflection of what's going on in his home life. This is a great way to collect data about a potential leader.

It has become very obvious to me that when evaluating a potential leader, one must go slowly in their evaluation. One of the primary reasons why is because you must give chance for situations to arise in order to gain an understanding of who you are dealing with and what kind of person you are considering joining your team. Especially in marriage.

There is much research to draw from when considering a person that is married to possibly join your team. In this research I find that a solid marriage involves great communication. If a person you're considering has a marriage that is in jeopardy, it is worth looking into and analyzing this person before moving forward to place them over a whole division of ministry. The marriage problem could result from a person who has difficulties communicating. If the candidate has trouble communicating with his or her own spouse, then there could be trouble in the way that this same person communicates with his or her team. Again, when it comes to evaluating a situation like this, it's not that you're looking for trouble to eliminate someone, but what you are watching for is a person that will work through situations properly, through scripture. The test will come, the storm will come, but it is a matter of how you handle the situation that will show who you are as a person.

As I pastored a church plant for almost thirteen years in the Northwest Ohio area, my own marriage was tested privately, and publicly. There is not one marriage that is perfect, and without challenges, and sometimes challenges beyond measure. The fact is that being in leadership in ministry, you are a target, and placed in the middle of the ring with Satan. The enemy tries to set up roadblocks, and barriers while trying to prevent you from doing the will of God. The fact is, that marriage will be thoroughly tested even without being involved in spiritual leadership. So, in my case, Cheryl and I were being tested privately before we ever started in spiritual leadership. One of the biggest mistakes in my life was the fact that before I got married, my wife asked me to set up marriage counseling for the both of us to ensure a solid start to a great marriage. However, at age twenty-four, fresh out of college and with a brand-new career position at IBM Corporation, I declined marriage counseling in my lack of wisdom. The reason being is because I shared with my then fiancée, that I was taught well by my spiritual advisors and that I was a God fearing man. I assured her that we could work through any problem, because we were in love. What a huge mistake I made in ignorance.

At the time I made those statements to Cheryl, I had no idea that I would encounter some situations that I didn't know how to handle, and the additional problems that it would cause due to my lack of wise counsel. At the age of twenty-four, I had zero interest in becoming a pastor, and I had zero interest in becoming an evangelist like my father. However, approximately eight years later, God began to call me into the ministry when I attempted to run like Jonah. At the time, in my eighth year of marriage, Cheryl and I had learned to overlook serious red flags in our marriage that we needed to deal with. At this point, we really needed to address the root of some of our issues. By the time we planted a church together some eleven years into our marriage, we began to experience some attacks in our lives that we knew not of, and neither did we understand what we were dealing with and how to handle it. We basically just did the best we could by trying to solve our problems without any experienced or qualified help. We tried to fix things on our own, but it didn't work, because we never addressed the root of our problems from the start. So, our situation grew worse and worse. We literally tried our very best to solve our issues while our church was growing. Here we are as a young couple with no marriage counseling from the start, and no ministry pre-counseling from any Bishop or qualified leader before starting our Bible study which grew into a church in Northwest Ohio. In a short few years, our church ministry was nearing one hundred members in a difficult city to grow a church. Finally, in years eight and nine of our church plant, the bandages that we were using to cover our problems were providing no benefit to our situation. Satan amplified his attack on our marriage, in which, we had four beautiful children. As a family, we were all caught in the middle of a nightmare of a storm that caused all of us to become miserable, unhappy, and many times discouraged. Cheryl began to feel like an afterthought because her husband was so focused on every aspect of building the church. She didn't understand how to handle the situation. I certainly had no clue what affect that I was having on her, and what I was dealing with.

When the church was in the middle of a growth spurt, I would become so excited, that I would ignore the problems that were eating away at our marriage. At this time, I was wrong and didn't know it, but the church gradually became my first love, and my wife unfortunately took a back seat. This drove her into a tailspin nightmare where she didn't know where to turn. Sometimes I would run away from her and become busy to avoid discussions that I thought would become negative. The enemy begin to place in my mind that she's just a complainer, and so I would believe that and carry on, even knowing deep down inside, my relationship wasn't just right. This situation had gotten to a point where it was starting to become noticeable by the members of the church. Folks began to see the strain on our marriage. This consequently affected our leadership. The church was not fully at ease because they could feel the tension between their leaders, husband and wife.

Our situation would not improve, even though we tried to communicate and work things out. As we continued to move forward in the church, I noticed that the folks saw the heaviness on their pastor and began to turn sour on the wife. This made things worse for Cheryl. She not only had the weight from our marital problems, and leadership issues in the church, but now had become an enemy of those feeling sorry for the pastor. What a mess this was. I had no idea how to fix this. I prayed and prayed, and the attack seemed to stay, and stay. Finally, there was a breaking point. My wife left me personally, and the ministry publicly. She could no longer take the pressure anymore. At this point, the church was full of heaviness, and even some left the church. I didn't blame the ones that left because I thought to myself, if my pastor and his wife couldn't get it together, then I would have probably left that situation as well. I would have felt concerned that I wasn't sitting under good leadership. This was a great time of grief for myself, wife and children. What seemed to be a great family, with a bright future seemed to take on quite a nightmare. Now this is the point where God had me in a fire where I had to ask for help immediately. Before, I would never ask for help because I had too much pride to admit that I needed help in my marriage. However, God divincly connected me with experienced pastors, Dr. Bowen, and Pastor Greene, along with their wives who took time with me, my wife and church to counsel us and teach us how to handle church leadership and marriage challenges. The counseling and prayers helped Cheryl and I to regain our footing, and even the ministry recovered as well. From this fiery trial, we all became stronger, wiser, and better. Research also proved that many times a problem in private, will eventually come to the forefront to cause confusion and chaos. Therefore, it is important to take time in the evaluation process before considering and placing a person over a whole division of ministry. I must state that while I was in this stinking situation, God had crushed me to the point where I had no more pride. In addition to our situation, our parents, family, friends, bishops and pastors from the Pentecostal Assemblies of The World rushed to our support as well. Without going into much detail on this, I will just mention that the support that Cheryl and I received was incredible. Cheryl and I even registered for needed spiritual counseling sessions with folks that didn't know us, and after several months of being cooperative and going through the process, I personally was humbled beyond measure. My marriage which was headed south at a tremendous rate of speed, but thank God that he placed it on our hearts to pursue much needed wise counseling. This was actually our final step to determine if we could reconcile, and if our family unit could be saved. One important principle that I learned along the way, as God molded me in that fire, is that any type of pride is unacceptable to God, even if it's unintended. Believe me, God will pinpoint areas that needs to be addressed in your life, and this is what happened to me. I'll start with me. Counseling illuminated for me how often I'd been wrong in the way I handled decisions in many of the issues and problems we faced through the years. My errors only made matters worse for my spouse. As a matter of fact, as I began to dive deeper and deeper into this research, I started to see myself as problematic in many areas. For example, when I first began to pastor, my father would say that I wasn't ready yet. This made me frustrated to the point where I said, I'll show you!! Really, what my father was saying to me is the same truth that my research pointed out in speaking of a person who is ready for promotion or not. I came to realize later on that I was the guy who was picked off of the tree before the fruit was ripe. When I was picked off too early, a good bite into my fruit proved to be bitter, and a situation in my private, and public life that was bitter.

My wife received counseling as well where she also was humbled and learned where she erred in the relationship. We both were humbled beyond measure and although we lost many folks who were impatient with the trials that we were experiencing, the good news is that when we returned back to church, the folks that endured this with us were able to see God do a miraculous work in my family's lives. So many in the church were able to witness God turn things around and watch us return to a harmonious position once again as leaders. Although there's still much to work through in our lives, the credit belongs to God alone who assisted us throughout our trials. I must say that now we have a testimony. Now the folks that watched us understand that God is able to bring anyone through any situation. I thank God so much for showing me myself, and developing our family to be stronger, wiser, and better than before.

Once the Lord worked things out for us in our marriage, while we were leading the church in Northwest Ohio, he allowed us to pastor and reestablish our footing in that area another three years. This is when God spoke to my heart about resigning and turning over the leadership to another pastor that could carry on the work from there. In the meantime, Cheryl and I, and our children were able to relocate to Columbus, Ohio, sit with a respectable, and powerful leader, Bishop James W Gaiters, who was our pastor for three years. As Cheryl and I settled at his church for three years, he and his wife, Lady Gaiters provided further wise counsel and leadership to us. We were now in an atmosphere where we could further heal, catch our breath and get situated in a new city. Again, God placed upon my heart to start another church plant in our new city. It is also refreshing to know that our children, who are so talented, and gifted in the Lord, is standing by our side and they are helping us to build in this new assignment that God has divinely given to us.

Your Child's Behavior Tells What Kind of Leader You Are

As you monitor potential leaders to be considered in a lead position over a division or branch of your organization, it is always a good idea to base this principle on 1 Timothy 3:4,5, *"One that ruleth well his own house, having his children in subjection with all gravity; (For if a man knows not how to rule his own house, how shall he take care of the church of God?)"* These verses are speaking of what Paul shared with Timothy on how to evaluate leaders in the church. This is a very important principle that I have never given much thought to, but I believe it's a golden nugget to those who are in a position where you are considering whether to place a person over a division of your ministry or organization. This is an area that I never focused in on until after reading through important facts that Paul mentioned. Had I used this principle many years ago when I was pastoring in another city, it would have worked wonders for me, saving me time and grief as well. The scripture mentions that a person's children should be in subjection with all gravity. Without getting extensively detailed, the Bible is saying that overall, the potential leader's children should be very respectful to others, and especially those who are over them. Coming under leadership authority, and displaying good manners, and a good attitude shows that a child was raised properly. Is the child a good worker, and does he or she have a good temperament? These are some of the points that needs to be evaluated. As I worked in education management as a dean of students, some of my responsibilities entailed handling discipline, and developing a learning culture in the school. In a short six to seven months on the job, I learned very quickly that the majority of problem children had something very wrong with their parenting. When teachers would send their children to my office, I would begin to ask questions to probe why the child continues to operate off track instead of following directions to avoid major penalties. What I have discovered over ninety percent of the time is that the parenting is very suspect. There is no doubt in my mind that the child is behaving in a certain way because of how he's being raised at home. When the home life has no order, structure or love, you're going to continuously have kids act out in contrary behavior for the most part. I will admit however, that there are some situations where the parenting is solid, but the child still rebels against their authority. However, in a general sense many of the kids have simply given up because they have no hope at home. There are also many kids who fail in school and won't complete any work, but when you ask them why, you hear stories like, we haven't had electricity or water for two weeks. You hear how dad had a physical fight with mom, or dad left mom and moved to another city with another women.

I had a child mention to me that their family's water was shut off for several days, and that she hadn't been able to take showers. These stories made me cringe. I've witnessed family after family that have had multiple children and who have different dads and moms. This was the norm in the area that I served in.

I've also found on the other hand that the students who perform well, and have great attitudes come from families who have good solid values and resources. The major point here as Mr. Renner states, "A child mirrors what happens behind a family's closed doors." If you were to analyze this principle, you would find it to be true. For example, if I have a child in school that seems uninterested in his work, I always discover later after meeting the parent, that they're unconcerned as well.

So, when you have a potential leader that you are considering, ensure that you look closely at the person's children. There will be sometimes that you may have an extraordinary situation with a kid who rebels, but for the most part you can get a good idea of what you're getting by looking at the children's parents. One other point to be clear. When the Bible talks about the children being in subjection with all gravity, it's talking about your children who still live under your roof, and influence. If parents can't rule their children well at home, then what makes you think that they'll be able to be a successful divine kingdom leader?

CHAPTER 10

The Ultimate Spiritual Experience

A Jesus View of Leadership

The best model that you can follow is the example of Jesus, and how he led in His three years of earthly ministry. His leadership was simply defined as service. "The true leader is concerned primarily with the welfare of others, not with his own comfort or prestige." When speaking of certain responsibilities of a spiritual leader, Jesus represents the first example, which is service. Jesus represented ultimate service because he had so much concern for the welfare of others that he was willing to die for the sins of mankind.

The second responsibility of a spiritual leader is to live a disciplined life. This means that this person must be an example to the others that he is leading. Theologically speaking, if he has God's spirit on the inside, then he is equipped to produce good conduct, or fruit. The spiritual leader must have standards, and these standards come from the Bible.

As a scriptural reference and foundation on this point, I like to refer to First John 3: 8, 9 *"He that committeth sin is of the devil; for the devil sinneth from the beginning. For this purpose, the Son of God was* manifested, that he might destroy the works of the devil. Whosoever is born of God doth not commit sin; for his seed remaineth in him: and he cannot sin, because he is born of God."* These two scriptures are profound, as it pertains to the flesh versus the spirit. When one would read in verse eight where it says he that committeth sin is of the devil. We all know that we have sinned, but we also know that we are not of the devil. The key here is to not take this scripture at face value, but according to its context. As the New Testament is written in Greek, then the word committeth means, he who practices sin as a habit in his life. Or it is a person that produces fleshly conduct because he has a fleshly seed. The same goes for verse nine when John says, whosoever is born of God does not commit sin. Again, we all know that all have sinned, and come short of the glory of God. However, this verse according to context is not talking about the fact that you won't commit a sin, because we all know that even though we're saved we've had some failures, and have sinned. So, since we've sinned, does that mean that we're not saved? No. The scripture is saying that the person who is born of God will not habitually practice sin, because His seed remaineth in him, and he cannot practice sin. A true spiritual leader is born of God and has the nature that's needed for God to use him in kingdom leadership. So, in this case, the Holy Spirit will lead and guide the leader to apply discipline in his life. If he doesn't, then God will chasten him, or correct him through disciplinary means until he yields peaceable fruits of righteousness.

Providing guidance is the third responsibility of the spiritual leader. God ordains these kinds of leaders because His sheep needs to be managed and directed to Him. In order for the leader to lead, then he must be following God, if he is to lead folks in the right direction. A.W. Tozer, who is considered a great leader said, "The ideal leader is one who hears the voice of God, and beckons on as the voice calls him and them."

Paul said to the Corinthian church, follow me, as I follow Christ. D.E. Hoste says, "In a mission like ours, those guiding its affairs must be prepared to put up with waywardness and opposition and be able to desist from the courses of action which, though they may be intrinsically sound and beneficial, are not approved by some of those affected."

The final principle is that the spiritual leader must take initiative. When you know that God is in control, and that He is the one who empowered you, and ordained your assignment, then there should be no hesitation about moving forward in faith. You cannot lead tentatively, but you must lead with bravery.

"More failure comes from an excess of caution than from bold experiments with new ideas. A friend who filled an important global post in Christian outreach recently remarked that when he surveyed his life, most of his failures came from insufficient daring. The frontiers of the kingdom of God were never advanced by men and women of caution." The key to this principle is being courageous, and not fearful, but full of faith, knowing that God is with you, and that there is no failure in God. Launch out into the deep, and make things happen.

THE EFFECTIVE SPIRITUAL LEADER

Once you are chosen to be promoted into an important level of leadership in the church, or any organization, it is important to realize that what you do in private will shine out in public. There are so many people who are in leadership roles in the church, but don't think about the impact that they should be making in the lives of God's people. It was mentioned in the previous section that spiritual leaders are to be servants, and a good example of showing discipline in their lives.

I believe it is vital that if folks are going to be effective in their leadership roles, then they're going to have to spend quality time with God. Psalms 16:11 says, *"In thy presence is fullness of joy; at thy right hand there are pleasures for evermore."* The difference between spiritual leadership and natural leadership is the devotional time spent with God, who strengthens us through the Holy Spirit. For example, as a Pastor who has to get in front of people to teach and preach to everyone, it is important for me to be anointed. If I'm not anointed by the Holy Spirit, then my words would be just empty words. The spiritual leader should steal away, and pray, seeking God's face. A person that doesn't spend time in the presence of God, will most likely be an empty person with no spiritual authority. The power comes from the quality time spent with the

Lord in prayer. Regarding the great spiritual leader Samuel Chadwick, it was said: "He was essentially a man of prayer. He was mighty in public prayer because he was constant in private devotion."

This is the way to become an effective influencer publicly. It is to go into a private area where you can spend unlimited time with God in order to receive strength, and anointing. A miserable, unhappy, and unmotivated leader is one that doesn't have a prayer life, one that doesn't communicate regularly with the Lord. To receive direction, and know the will of God, and to hear His voice takes being in His presence on a regular basis. If one observes closely, you find that a leader's private life will show publicly. If that person spends not much time with God, there will be no anointing, and there will be no power. All it takes is watching a person closely, and you will be able to sense a person's heart for God. Why? Always remember, that you know them by their fruits. In my experience of being around many different types of leaders in the church, I notice how some leaders are more spiritual than others. The key is to always watch the fruit. Usually what they practice is who they are. If they always do carnal things, then you know that that leader is not spiritual, and not as anointed. When you observe a person that loves the Lord, and always does things to impact the kingdom, then you'll know that their fruits are spiritual.

Now this leads me to an important area that is critical to spiritual leadership in the church, prayer. If you are to be a leader of influence, then you must pray more than the folks who you are trying to influence. Many times, as pastors, we will do much talking about the power of prayer, and even folks in the pews will talk about the power of prayer, but really, it's mostly talk. If you ask the average person to be honest and share how much they pray, you will find that there won't be many that can boast about it. Through the years I would say to our church, if only you knew how prayer is working on your behalf, you would pray more.

I believe one of the primary reasons that prayer is a challenge for many people is because they don't understand spiritually how it is working for their good in a powerful way. Before his death, respected man of God Samuel Chadwick said that he wished that he had prayed more. This is a man who was known as a prayer warrior, a man who prayed constantly. One of the excuses that folks will use, I do not pray like I should because of my busy schedule. In life many times we find time to do things that are important to us, but often we avoid putting things like prayer in a primary position of importance.

Every day, I rise up early in the morning to make it to the office on time. However, there are many occasions where I will rise even earlier at 5am to get a brief work out at the health club, before going to the office. When I arrive to the health club to park, I notice that the parking lot is full of cars to the point that sometimes I have to park further from the door because of limited spaces. The first thing that comes to my mind is, I bet if it were 5am prayer, this lot wouldn't be as filled with as many cars.

What I am saying is that folks will make all kinds of excuses about why they don't pray more, but when it comes to getting their bodies into shape, then that takes priority. People don't even realize how horrible this can appear spiritually. It actually appears as if the natural is more important than the spiritual. The question becomes, would I rather have a wonderful built up body, over a closer fellowship with God? No contest!

This means that priorities must change. It is always important to look at the example of Jesus. He spent much time in prayer, so if Jesus had to spend much time in prayer, then we should realize the importance of prayer if we are to be spiritually fit. J. Oswald Sanders shares the point that "Prayer kept Jesus' moral vision sharp and clear. Prayer gave him courage to endure the perfect but painful will of His Father." Oswald points out how the principle of prayer was used by Jesus, even in His decision-making process. Before he selected candidates in for spiritual leadership, he went into prayer in Luke 6:12. I'll reinforce Oswald's point here; Prayer is hard work. He says it here, "True intercession is a sacrifice, a bleeding sacrifice. We see Jesus in Hebrews 5:7 offer up prayers and petitions with loud cries and tears, but afterwards performed great miracles."

Prayer is a strenuous exercise, as we wrestle over circumstances that we are dealing with or when we're interceding on behalf of someone else. So, it is good to ask God to search our hearts and nourish our spirit to be able to do His will. Although prayer is a physical activity, we are to pray in the spirit. That is, yielding ourselves totally to the leading, and feeding of God's spirit.

Our hearts must be right with God when we pray. We must approach His throne through Jesus Christ our mediator. One other important key that Oswald mentions, and something that many people fail to do is wait and listen for God to speak to our hearts. A spiritual leader will pray in the spirit, by yielding to the spirit with a clean heart through Jesus Christ the justifier, which is why we can come boldly to the throne of grace. At the same time, teaching must take place on waiting and listening to God. Another power of prayer is to combat Satan. Prayer is the most effective spiritual assault weapon in our arsenal, and it must be used in this day against many false prophets that are rising. It must be used against the evil influence of Satan and must push back the powers of darkness. It will push back darkness if we're sincere, in constant prayer, believing that God will work on our behalf.

The objective of Satan is to cause the saint of God to become depressed, miserable, unhappy, and discouraged. However, the power of prayer must be exercised to overcome the trick of the enemy. The way to fight in the spirit of prayer, is applying our faith. Our faith is applied by refusing to be overwhelmed by the wiles of the devil, but at the same time, pray with expectation that God will fix things on your behalf. Prayer will move God on your behalf. Prayer will move Satan out of your way as a barrier, and your prayers will move the people. Don't forget to even pray for your people, believing you will experience the mighty hand of God to deliver you in spiritual warfare. Remember, Ephesians 6:12, *"For we wrestle not against flesh and blood, but against principalities, against powers, against the rulers of the darkness of this world, against spiritual wickedness in high places."* The spiritual leader must operate in the spirit, and prayer must be the weapon that is used to overcome the satanic influence. Any conflict that you face as a leader, or any decision that you make as a leader, prayer must be the primary focus of a successful leader.

THE MIND AND VISION OF A SPIRITUAL LEADER

We have examined one of the key factors behind the motivation of a spiritual leader. When God raises up leaders for His kingdom, He specifically starts with the heart. Once a person's heart is opened to God, committed, and submitted to the work of the kingdom, the Lord begins to develop you into the servant that you are to be. He takes you through experiences, test, and trials to prepare you for the great task that lies in front of you to lead and advance His kingdom. Once the heart is dealt with, God also has to deal with your mind. This is one aspect that I will focus on in this part of the research. When it comes to salvation, God always start with the heart, in pouring out His spirit within man freely by His grace. Thus, the mind follows the heart's desires. I will always make it a must, to base my opinions, revelations from God, and principles I share based upon scripture. In my studies of the Servant Leader by Blanchard and Hodges, I am totally in agreement with the scripture provided to provide foundation for the points that I'd like to share. Romans 12:2 says, *"And be not conformed to this world: but be ye transformed by the renewing of your mind, that ye may prove what is that good, and acceptable, and perfect, will of God."*

Now that your heart and mind has been transformed, a person should be able to fulfill the will of God for his life. When it comes to pastoring, or leading an organization, you may have knowledge, passion, and resources, but one of the primary ingredients that's needed in order to be successful is vision. If you don't have vision, you won't go very far. Once you are called by God to lead, and He equips you, in order to lead others, it's going to take vision. In order to influence others, they will have to understand, and buy into the goals that are to be accomplished. Notice what is said in Proverbs 29:18, *"Where there is no vision, the people perish: but he that keepeth the law, happy is he."*

Passion and vision are the key factors to determine whether you can be successful in leading your organization. If the people are not excited about the future then, how can you ever grow? Some great research here is giving important insight to what I even need to do as a pastor in leading my church. Of course, we've already determined that if your church is going to grow, it will take a great deal of spending time with God in prayer and being a good servant leader.

What I am realizing and learning more, is that servant leadership is not about letting people do what they please, and you support them, but being a servant leader is about doing the right thing and doing things right. Jesus had a vision when He led, and He also displayed great influence, and excitement about the future with his followers. So, this is the same thing that you must do in order to influence and move the people you are leading.

In the book, The Servant Leader, "leadership and vision are terms that are used to convey a message of how to effectively lead God's people just like Jesus did." In the most simplistic way, I will share what needs to be done effectively to lead the people. How will you benefit the people? Where are you going? What are your standards? This is what is called leadership vision. You as a leader can answer all of these great questions, and provide answers about what your vision is, but the key is that the people must also be as passionate about what you're doing as you are. If the folks are not excited, then how can you grow? This is where prayer comes in, because you must ask the Lord to show you specifically how to influence the people. When it comes to divine kingdom leadership, your people should be so excited about the vision that they forget about themselves and concentrate more on God and His business of saving souls. The thing to remember is to have a clear vision that your people are excited about.

As I've worked in the school system as a dean of students there is something that I always try to remind teachers of every chance I get. That is, when the job becomes stressful, and some of the students will not come under your authority of leadership, before you throw the book at them and give up, just think why you are in this position. I say this because there are some students who are incredibly hard to deal with. They will talk back disrespectfully in defiance and will become insubordinate.

Most of the time, it is because of bad parenting, along with students wanting to show off in front of other kids in their classroom. I watch teachers many times check these kids totally off and give up hope. That's when I remind them of our goals, and mission. I remind them that we were hired to educate students and teach them how to become productive citizens in society. I always remind teachers to give students chances to redeem themselves, and chances to overcome mistakes. This will also give them something to reach for. This gives them a vision, and it also helps you fulfil your mission. When the mission is clear, it helps to keep the passion in the leader, and the followers.

My point is that when pastors lead churches and work to keep the vision in the forefront of both their own heart as well as those of their people then as we experience challenging situations, it will be a great reminder about the work that we are doing in the kingdom. If you are in the business of guiding people to Jesus so that their lives can be transformed, then we must deal with these folks based on your mission. Of course, there will be some extraordinary situations to happen where there are certain people you have to simply walk away from.

Many times folks in leadership operate without vision, and end up ruling over people, when the Bible clearly indicates that the Lord doesn't want you to "Lord over His people, but being examples unto them," 1 Peter 5:3. Being a servant leader is not being a people pleaser, but it is doing things right, and doing things the right way, and being examples unto the Lord's people. This is the principle that everyone must grasp from and put into operation.

When implementing the vision to your followers, it is important to show them what the future looks like. In other words, make it clear to them the type of impact that you would like to make in the lives of God's people. As you paint the picture of the future, it is just as important to share your values and make them clear as well. They should know the rank of your values. For example, God first, family, and other values. I've learned hard lessons that ministry starts in the home. In the past, there have been so many leaders that made the mistake of reaching out to others so much so that they forget to minister to their own family. After years go by, you then see the mess that has developed in your own family when they are not valued first.

Even Jesus valued his teaching toward his disciples. In Matthew 22:37-40, His example says, *"Jesus said unto him, thou shalt love the Lord thy God with all thy heart, and with all thy soul, and with all thy mind. This is the first and greatest commandment. And the second is like unto it, "thou shalt love thy neighbor as thyself."* If a leader can use these principles in the way that he handles his followers, then he will achieve great success. When a leader can inject vision, and direction, the best way to influence the people who follow you is to live it in front of them. Be an example.

Now, this next point is so dear to me, and I'm grateful that it was covered in this research. One thing that really concerns me, is when I see Christian organizations primarily focus on the leaders, but not the people. I've been to fellowship church meetings and services where many times the focus of the worship service were about leader elevations and celebrating them. I am all for celebrating leaders, especially when they are worthy of elevation. However, I suggest that it's not a good idea to get carried away with spending too much time on this type of activity. There's nothing wrong with celebrating a worthy candidate in a service, but it could end up being a subtle distraction from the main point of the worship service which is introducing Jesus Christ to lost souls. If we spend too much time on the celebration of a candidate, we can miss our goal of ministering to someone who needs to be saved or touched by God. There is so much a stake when it comes to ministering the gospel to lost souls. Leaders simply cannot forgot about the people in the sanctuary. When you have a self-serving leader, his primary concern is about his title, and authority of Lording over God's people. This is the part of the goal where a divine kingdom leader must carefully lead by example, according to the example Jesus displayed in His earthly ministry which primarily revealed His humility. One of the most powerful quotes in this research came from the book, The Servant Leader. I was so thrilled to see that the authors could make this so understandable, because this is a major problem in the church today.

I will list a great portion of this quote, because I believe it needs to be made aware to every leader who has a heart to serve in the kingdom. "Living according to the vision, is where most leaders get into trouble. The traditional hierarchy too often is kept alive and well, leaving the people neglected at the bottom. All the energy in the organization moves up the hierarchy as workers try to please and be responsive to their bosses. In this environment, self-serving leaders assume that the sheep are there for the benefit of the shepherd. All the energy in the organization flows up the hierarchy."

This is a big negative! This point of view needs to be flipped, where the leader should be responsive to the followers. The goal is for the leader to help them accomplish the vision, and direction of the organization which should be leading them to Jesus

Christ. Jesus showed by example the proper thing to do which was demonstrating to the people that I (Jesus) am willing to wash the feet of my disciples. Jesus made it very clear that he didn't come to be served, but to serve, Matthew 20:28. He actually came to serve the vision that God had given him for the kingdom. This folks is what true servant leadership is about. It is about a leader that is selfless and comes to the aid of God's people to direct them to the vision, and mission that God has revealed to them. God doesn't ask us to die for our followers, but he ask His leaders to make the vision clear and lead the people by example to help them accomplish the goal.

Divine kingdom leadership is bigger than you, and in order to do things God's way, the leader must have a heart that's ready, and willing to be a servant. I grew up a son of a pastor, and inter-national evangelist, so I've seen so many different situations in the church in a general sense.

I recall attending an international church convention where there were worship services every evening through the week. I remember one weekday evening, Cheryl and I went to a service that started off with sincere praise and worship in which there were about five thousand people worshipping God. There was a powerful move of God in the service. But, all of a sudden, the music stopped, and the worship eased up, because the Bishops were walking in. All of the people were instructed to rise out of their seats in honor of the Bishops who walked down the aisle of the service up towards the stage. Once they reached the stage, it seemed to me that the rest of the service was focused on the bishops, ceremonial consecrations, and elevations. These ceremonial and consecration activities are needed, but I believe that the timing of them should be considered. I don't believe that it should happen in the middle of a worship service where it causes worship of the people to God to cease. I believe it should happen before worship starts so that there is a corporate worship without interruption. This, of course, is my humble opinion.

In my humble opinion, I believe in honoring, serving and coming under the authority of any bishop of the Lord Jesus Christ that is appointed over me. I honor my bishops, respect them greatly, and love them dearly, however, just because bishops walk into the worship service, my worship to God shouldn't ever cease. Corporate worship in the spirit ceased in my particular experience that I witnessed, and the focus shifted to the bishops for the rest of the service until the sermon. I believe that the people were forgotten in terms of them having an opportunity to be strengthened in worship. The ones who were supposed to be strengthened and directed to the vision of surrendering to Jesus Christ were suddenly forgotten because it was celebration time. Therefore, this research is so important for future leaders in the kingdom. Primary focus must always remain on God. Spiritual leaders should make an effort to place God as the absolute priority in every worship service. No glory, or focus should be stolen away from God. "Servant leadership requires a level of intimacy with the needs and aspirations of the people being led that might be beyond the level of intimacy an ego-driven leader is willing to sustain."

Always remember, there will be many leaders who are well accomplished in their personal lives and may seem to get great results of success from our humanistic viewpoint. However, if he or she is not an example of the servant leader, then you can discount any result you may see, and begin to search and pray for a servant leader that you can follow safely. In the Old Testament, the magicians also performed many of the miracles that Moses performed, but in the end, their tricks couldn't stand up to the authentic power of the Holy Spirit. Many are called, but the chosen are few - Matthew 22:14.

CHAPTER 11

Marriage Encounter Thoughts & Conclusion

I'm grateful to God that he would place on my heart to conduct a research study, along with sharing my own personal experiences on divine kingdom leadership. The wealth of information that we covered in this research and from my experience is sure to enlighten anyone who aspires to be an effective leader in God's kingdom. When it comes to spiritual leadership, this is one of the most powerful, and important assignments in life, because it's dealing with God's chosen people. When I think of the type of information that was learned within this research, it makes me think about marriage. Anyone who has plans to get married should also make certain that substantive marriage counseling is on the schedule before joining in holy matrimony. I've made many mistakes in my life, but there are two mistakes that really stand out. The first mistake was to refuse marriage counseling. I made the decision to marry my beautiful wife, and she desired marriage counseling, but I didn't. I thought, well, I've grown up in church, I love the Lord, I'm sincere, and open minded enough to work out any problem that we may have in the future. That was one of the worse thoughts that ever came to my mind, and one of the worse assumptions I've ever had.

When our marriage ran into major challenges, I had no idea how I should have handled the issues. All I did was make things worse, and worse in trying to fix things on my own. It wasn't until a major crisis took place, that I realized that our relationship, and our future together was in jeopardy. Our problems seemed beyond our ability to solve.

Thank God, however, for experienced spiritual counselors that supported us and guided us during the course of our marriage when facing a time period of difficulty. God miraculously used these anointed leaders to help us reconcile with one another. The Lord also strengthened our faith walk with Him, as well. Cheryl and I learned so much about ourselves, negative & positive. Our growth spiritually was exponential. The strategy of Satan to dismantle us was clearly revealed to us as we overcame our trouble. One point that stands out to me is the spiritual leadership of our counselors. They applied scripture, prayer, love, experience and knowledge to our circumstances. I must say, those leaders were chosen by God to lead in His kingdom. The result of this divine leadership saved our marriage, family, children, and future. During this time, it came to me, what a mistake I made in the first place, by not receiving the proper training, and pre-counseling needed before we started our journey. This my friends, was one of the most humbling lessons in my life.

My second mistake was the fact that when I felt the leading of the Lord to plant my first church, I should have sought my father's advice first. My pride told me that I could do it, but I should have told my pride to shut up! I should have pursued the necessary pastoral and leadership training before getting started to understand what to look for. Although I had some limited training by my father and other pastors that I was associated with, it took several years to realize the magnitude of my mistakes and my lack of training and preparedness. Although I did a decent job in my pastoral assignment, and although we had a vibrant church, I could have avoided some unwanted headaches that troubled our family. I simply needed pastoral counseling and training before starting the ministry. It's always the best idea to take your time and move slow. Building something magnificent takes time. Just because one can sing a little, teach and preach doesn't mean he's ready for pastoral promotion. I continue to constantly need sharpening and wise council. Everyone should always stay updated in learning as much as we can to make a positive impact in the kingdom. When our church faced its first real threat of serious challenges, this is when I decided that I simply needed help. As I began to soul search for answers regarding experiences that I'd already had or was facing, God touched my heart to lead me to do research on Divine Kingdom Leadership. The data that I've gathered within this research study has been so phenomenally incredible and revealed to me what I was missing. Now, I'm ready to lead with purpose, experience, structure, and with spiritual standards. After years of trying to do this on my own, I now realize that my way is not good enough, but God's way produces advancements, and excellence in His kingdom. I'm now better prepared, and better equipped more than ever.

Research proves that becoming a spiritual leader is a call from God, and you must be regenerated by His Spirit in order to be considered a child of God or qualified to lead. There are so many that will tell you that they are a believer, born again, and washed in the blood of Jesus, but until they pass the acid test, they can't be considered authentic. This same principle can be applied to leadership.

This research information also proves that Jesus Christ is the best example to use as a model to follow. We must not only read what He says in His word, but we must strive to operate in principles that He used. The scripture that best represents this research is Matthew 23:11, *but he that is greatest among you shall be your servant*. This is how Jesus sees things. The Lord calls you to ministry, and gives you a message, and field of service. A person cannot just go out and fulfill a high level of spiritual responsibility without the Holy Spirit working within. There are folks that go into ministry because they have the wrong view of what it's all about. Some desire to be celebrities. Some desire to be glorified. They don't realize that this is a servant's work.

The true servant of God is disciplined in their kingdom assignment and are hard to find. It is a must that leadership in ministry is conducted with the right heart, and that your ambition doesn't steal any glory away from the almighty God. One of the most powerful principles in this research was drawn from the ten guidelines to tell if a person was ready for promotion. When it comes to evaluating spiritual leadership, even though you might be called, you may not be ready yet. God has His leaders in a process of development so that they will reach the point where they can be used as instruments in His hands. It takes so much of giving yourself to the Lord to be considered a divine kingdom leader. It is a must that we spend much time with God, so that we can be spiritually empowered with revelation and anointing. A spiritual leader led by God is one who is on a mission to change lives and become a major influence in the lives of God's people. In divine kingdom leadership, you never arrive, because there is always something to learn, and this is why a spiritual leader remains humble, constantly striving to be in the presence of the Lord. God's kingdom must be advanced, and Godly leadership is needed. The leader must have the right heart. God starts with the heart and Nehemiah provides a wonderful example how the Lord empowered him to influence change in his era. I believe that this research information targeted for successful leadership can be applied not only in a church organization, but in any business that desires to operate in efficiency, integrity and excellence. I'm so grateful, and thankful to God for this wonderful teaching that I have received. I will certainly use this material for teaching in the years to come and will work to develop up and coming leaders in the body of

Christ. I will always be forever grateful to my late father, who took the time to share his detailed experiences he accumulated, and what God has taught him through the years. It's always a good idea to take instruction from someone who has gone before you. This, my friends will save you from so much headache, problems, and difficulties. Those with experience and wisdom have already traveled the road that is new to those who are younger. It will never hurt you to pause and listen. Listening could be the greatest blessing and revelation in your life. There's no doubt in my mind that God supernaturally led me to research this subject of divine kingdom leadership. This research study has been life changing for me and will have an indelible impact on me for the rest of my life. My prayer is that whoever has the opportunity to go through this study will realize the unbelievable privilege it is to serve in the kingdom of God.

Bibliography

Blanchard, Ken and Hodges, Phil. (2003). *The Servant Leader: Transforming Your Heart, Head, Hands & Habits*. Nashville, TN: Thomas Nelson, Inc.

Cutshall, Brian. (2005). *Where Are the Armor Bearers: Strength and Support for Spiritual Leaders*. Cleveland, Tennessee: Pathway Press.

Nance, Terry. (1990). *God's Armor Bearer: How to Serve God's Leaders*. Little Rock, AR: Published by Focus on the Harvest.

Renner, Rick. (2000). *Promotion: Ten Guidelines To Help You Achieve Your Long-Awaited Promotion*. Tulsa, OK: New Edition (2005), Teach All Nations Publishing, a division of Rick Renner Ministries

Sanders, J. Oswald. (2007). *Spiritual Leadership: A Commitment to Excellence for Every*

Believer. Chicago, IL: Moody Publishers.

Tripp, Paul David. (2002). *Instruments in the Redeemer's Hand: People in Need of Change, Helping People in Need of Change*. Phillipsburg, NJ: P&R Publishing.

White, James Emery. (2011). *What They Didn't Teach You in Seminary: 25 lessons for Successful Ministry in Your Church*. Grand Rapids, MI: Baker Books, a division of Baker Publishing Group.